Friedrich Schiller

Schiller's Ballads

A literal translations

Friedrich Schiller

Schiller's Ballads
A literal translations

ISBN/EAN: 9783744792691

Printed in Europe, USA, Canada, Australia, Japan

Cover: Foto ©Thomas Meinert / pixelio.de

More available books at **www.hansebooks.com**

Handy Literal Translations

Schiller's Ballads

A LITERAL TRANSLATION

HINDS & NOBLE, Publishers

4 COOPER INSTITUTE   NEW YORK CITY

CONTENTS.

(v)

SCHILLER'S BALLADS.

THE DIVER.

"Who dares, knight or servant, to dive into
 this abyss? I throw down a golden cup,
 already has the black mouth swallowed it.
 He who can show me the cup again may   5
 keep it, it is his own."

The king speaks, and from the height of the
 cliff, which reaches out rugged and steep
 into the endless sea, he hurls the cup into   10
 the howling Charybdis. "Who is the courageous one, I ask again, to dive down into
 this depth?"

And the knights and the servants round about
 him hear it and remain silent; they look   15
 down into the wild sea, but no one desires
 to win the cup. And the king again
 the third time asks: "Is there no one
 who dares to go down?"

(1)

But everyone remains silent as before; and 20
a page, gentle and bold, steps forth out of
the trembling body of the servants, and
throws off his girdle, and his mantle, and
all the men and women round about look
in wonder upon the beautiful youth.

And as he steps to the brink of the rock, and 25
looks down into the abyss, Charybdis gave
back, howling, the waters which she had
swallowed and as with the roaring of dis- 30
tant thunder they rush foaming forth
from the dark abyss.

And it foams and seethes and roars and hisses,
as when water mingles with fire. Even to
heaven rises the steaming spray, and flood 35
presses on flood in endless succession, and
seems never to wish to exhaust or empty
itself, as though the sea were about to give
birth to another sea.

But finally the wild force calms itself, and
black in the midst of the white foam there
gapes a yawning cleft, bottomless, as 40
though it went to the realm of hell, and
raging one sees the boiling waves drawn
down into the whirling funnel.

Now quickly before the surf returns, the youth
  commends himself to God, and—a cry of 45
  horror is heard round about, and already
  the whirlpool has washed him away, and
  mysteriously over the bold swimmer the
  jaw closes itself; he shows himself no
  longer.

And it becomes silent over the watery abyss,
  only from the depth it roars hollowly, and 50
  trembling one hears from mouth to mouth:
  "Highhearted youth, farewell!" And
  hollower and hollower one hears it howling, and yet they wait with fearful, terrible
  waiting.

And were you to throw the crown itself in 55
  there, and were you to say: Whoever
  brings me the crown, he shall wear it and
  shall be king! I would have no desire for
  the dear reward. Whatever the howling
  deep down there may conceal, that no liv- 60
  ing happy soul will tell.

Well many a vessel, seized by the whirlpool,
  shot headlong down into the deep; but
  only the shattered keel and mast reached
  forth out of the all-consuming grave.—
  And clearer and clearer, like the roar of 65
  a storm, one hears it roaring ever nearer
  and nearer.

And it foams and seethes and roars and hisses,
  as when water mingles with fire ; even to
  heaven rises the foaming spray, and wave   70
  presses on wave in endless succession, and
  as the roar of distant thunder, it pours
  forth howling out of the dark abyss.

And see ! out of the dark watery abyss, something raises itself white as a swan, and an   75
  arm, and a gleaming neck becomes bare, and
  some one swims with strength and with
  eager diligence ; it is he, and high in his
  left hand he swings the cup with joyous
  beckoning.

And long he breathed and deep and greeted the   80
  heavenly light. With cries of joy one
  called to the other : " He lives ! he is there !
  It did not keep him ! Out of the grave, out
  of the whirling cave of waters the brave one
  has saved his soul alive."

And he comes ; and the rejoicing throng sum-   85
  mons him ; he sinks at the feet of the king,
  kneeling he offers him the cup ; and the
  king beckons to his lovely daughter ; she fills
  it to the brim with sparkling wine, and the   90
  youth thus addresses the king :

"Long live the king! Let him rejoice whoever breathes under the rosy light! But
   down there it is terrible, and let not man
   tempt the gods, and let him never, nay   95
   never, desire to see what they graciously
   cover with night and horror.

" It drew me down with lightning's speed; then
   from a rocky shaft there rushed against me
   a wild, raging fountain; the furious power 100
   of the undertow seized me, and like a top
   it drove me about with dizzy turning; I
   could not resist.

"Then God, to whom I called, in my greatest,
   most terrible need, showed to me a cliff 105
   reaching out of the deep; this I quickly
   seized, and escaped death. And there too
   hung the cup on sharp corals, otherwise it
   would have fallen into the bottomless abyss.

"For beneath me it lay yet mountain deep in 110
   purple darkness, and although here, as far
   as the eye was concerned, there was eternal
   sleep, the eye looked down with shuddering,
   as there moved salamanders and cuttlefish
   and dragons in the terrible jaw of hell.

"Black moved there, in gruesome mixture, 115
   rolled up into horrible balls, the prickly
   roach, the horrible malformed figure of the
   hammerfish, and the terrible shark, the
   hyena of the sea, threatening showed me 120
   his fierce-looking teeth.

"There I hung and was conscious to myself
   with a shudder, under masks, the only feeling heart, so far from human help, alone in
   the awful solitude, far beneath the sound of 125
   human speech, by the gruesome creatures of
   the sad desert.

" And with a shudder I thought this, and then
   something crept near, moving a hundred
   limbs at once, and was about to snap at
   me ; in the fever of terror I let go the coral 130
   branch that I had seized ; and immediately
   the whirlpool seized me with a mad tumult ;
   but it was my salvation, for it drew me
   upward."

The king was astonished at this and speaks :
   "The cup is thine, and this ring also I 135
   promise you, adorned with the most costly
   stones, if you will try once more, and will
   bring me news of what you saw on the
   deepest part of the sea bottom."

This the daughter heard with tender feeling,
and with flattering lips she plead : " Father, 140
let this be enough of the cruel sport ! He has
endured for you what no other one endures,
and if you cannot tame the desires of your
heart, why then the knights may outdo the
servant." •

Upon this the king quickly seizes the cup, and 145
hurls it into the whirlpool, saying : " And
if you bring me back the cup, you shall be
my noblest knight, and this very day, as a 150
husband, you shall embrace her who now
pleads for you with tender pity."

Then his soul is seized with a heavenly power,
and his eyes gleam with a bold light, and
he sees the beautiful form blush, and grow
pale, and sink down ; he feels impelled to 155
gain the costly prize, and plunges down for
life or death.

Now one hears the surf, now it returns again,
the thundering sound announces it ; then
they bend down with loving look, they come, 160
the waters all come, they rush up, they
rush down, but none of them brings the
youth again.

THE GLOVE.

Before his arena, waiting for the games, sat
    king Francis, and round about him the
    great ones of the realm, and in a circle upon   5
    the high balcony sat the ladies, like a beau-
    tiful wreath.

And as he beckons with his finger the wide door
    is opened, and in steps a lion with thought-
    ful air, and silently he looks round about   10
    himself, yawning for some time ; he shakes
    his mane, stretches his limbs, and lays him- 15
    self down.

And the king motions again ; then quickly a
    second door is opened, out of it with a wild 20
    leap runs a tiger. As he sees the lion he
    roars aloud, beats with his tail a terrible

circle, stretches his tongue and shyly he   25
he circles around, the lion angrily pursuing,   30
and growling he then stretches himself at
his side.

And the king beckons again, then the doubly
opened cage sends forth two leopards at   35
once. These pounce with courageous desire
for contest upon the tiger ; it seizes them
with its fierce claws, and the lion with a
roar arises, and then silence ensues ; and   40
round in a circle the fierce animals, hot with
murderous desire, stretch themselves.

Then from the parapet's edge there falls a glove   45
from a beautiful hand, right between the
tiger and the lion.

And with a scorning manner, Miss Cunigund
turns to knight Delorges : " Sir knight, if   50

your love is so fiery, as you swear it to me
every hour, then pick up my glove.''

And the knight with speedy course stepped
down into the terrible cage with firm tread 55
and out of the midst of the terrible creatures
he takes the glove with bold·hand.

And with astonishment and horror the knights
and noble ladies see it ; and calmly he brings 60
back the glove.   Then his praise resounds
from every lip, but with tender look of
love—it promises approaching happiness—
Miss Cunigund receives him.   And he 65
throws the glove into her face :—'' Your
thanks, lady, I desire not !'' and he leaves
her that selfsame hour.

THE RING OF POLYCRATES.

He stood at the edge of his roof; with well
pleased heart he looked down upon the over-
ruled Samos.   '' All this is subject to me,''
began he to the king of Egypt.   '' Acknowl- 5
edge that I am happy.''

" You have experienced the pleasure of the gods !
Those who were formerly your equals, them
the power of your scepter now rules. But 10`
one still lives to avenge himself ; my mouth
cannot pronounce you happy while yet the
enemy's eye is watching."

And even before the king had ended, a messenger
sent from Miletus placed himself before 15
the tyrant : " Sir, let the fragrance of the
sacrifice arise, and crown thy festive hair
with joyous laurel twigs !

"Overcome by the spear sank thy foe, thy 20
faithful general Polydor sends me with the
joyful tale—" and out of a black vessel, to
the horror of both, he takes forth a well-
known, still bloody head.

The king steps back with horror. " But I warn 25·
you against trusting fortune," he exclaims
with troubled look. " Think, upon faith-
less waves—how easily can the storm shatter
it—floats the doubtful fortune of thy 30
fleet."

And even before he had spoken the words, the
    rejoicing has interrupted him, resounding
    from the anchorage.   Richly laden with
    foreign treasures the fleet, abounding in   35
    masts like a forest, returns homeward to its
    own docks.

The royal guest is astonished : ''Thy fortune
    to-day is well disposed, but fear thou its
    inconstancy.   The throngs of Cretans well   40
    trained in arms threaten you with the perils
    of war ; already are they near to this
    .strand.''

And even before the words had fallen from his
    lips, one sees a throng coming from the
    ships, and a thousand voices cry : '' Victory !   45
    We are freed from the presence of the foe ;
    the storm has destroyed the Cretans, it is
    past, the war is gone ! ''

This the guest friend hears with terror.   '' Truly   50
    I must esteem thee happy ! but,'' says he,
    '' I tremble for thy welfare.   I shudder at the
    envy of the gods.   The unmixed joy of life
    was awarded to no earth-born one.

"I too succeeded in everything, in all my acts of   55
    government the favor of heaven accom-
    panied me ; but I had a dear son ; him God
    took from me, I saw him die, I paid my   60
    debt to fortune.

"Therefore if you would protect yourself from
    misfortune, plead with the invisible ones,
    that they may grant you grief with your
    joy. None yet have I seen ending happily
    upon whom the gods strew their gifts with   65
    hands ever full.

"And if the gods do not grant it, take warning
    at the teaching of a friend, and call upon
    misfortune yourself ; whatever of all your   70
    treasures may please your heart the most,
    that take and throw into the sea !"

And, moved by fear, he speaks : "Of all that
    this island holds, this ring is my greatest   75
    treasure. I will sacrifice it to the Furies ; .
    they may then pardon my good fortune,"
    and he throws the treasure into the flood.

And with the light of the following morning,
   with joyous face a fisherman appears before 80
   the ruler: "Sir, this fish have I caught,
   a better one than has ever before gone into
   my net; I bring it to you as a present."

And when the cook cuts up the fish, he jumps 85
   back with astonishment, and with surprised
   look he cries : "See, Sir, the ring which
   you carried ; I found it in the fish's stomach.
   Ah, thy fortune is boundless!" 90

At this the guest turns away in horror : "I cannot
   dwell here longer, you can be my friend no
   more. The gods desire thy destruction ; I 95
   hasten away, so as not to die with you."
   He spoke, and quickly went on board his
   ship.

SIR TOGGENBURG.

"Knight, true sister's love does this heart give
   to you, ask no other love, for it gives me
   pain."   "In silence can I bear to see you 5

coming, in silence see you going ; the silent
weeping of your eyes I cannot understand."

And he hears it with deep grief, bleeding he 10
    tears himself away, passionately embraces
    her, swings himself upon his horse, sends
    word to all his men in Switzerland ; they
    make a pilgrimage to the Holy Land.   Upon 15
    their breasts they wear the cross.

These perform great deeds with the arm of
    heroes ; the plumes of their helmets wave
    in the throngs of their foes ; and the name 20
    of the Toggenburger frightens the Mussul-
    man ; but the heart cannot recover from its
    grief.

A year has he borne it, he endures it no longer ; 25
    peace he cannot find and he leaves the army ;
    on Joppa's strand he sees a ship whose

sails are swelling ; he boards it, bound for   30
home to the dear native land where her
breath gently moves.

And at the gate of her castle the pilgrim knocks ,
Alas, with harsh words is it opened : "She   35
whom you seek carries the veil ; yesterday
was the anniversary of the day that betrothed   40
her to God."

Upon this he leaves forever the castle of his
father, his weapons he sees no more, nor his
faithful horse ; from Toggenburg he de-   45
scends, unknown, for a hairy garment covers
his noble limbs.

And he builds himself a hut near the place,   50
where out of the midst of gloomy linden-
trees the convent appears ; waiting from the

morning light to the evening's gleam, with   55
    quiet hopefulness upon his face, he sat
    there alone.

He looked to the convent over yonder, looked
    for hours to the window of his dear one,
    until the window sounded, until the lovely   60
    one showed herself, until the dear image
    bent down into the valley, softly, mild as an
    angel.

Then he joyfully laid himself down, went to   65
    sleep comforted, looking forward in quiet
    joy to the coming morn. And thus, he sat -
    there many days, sat there many years,   70
    waiting without pain or complaint,

Until the window sounded, until the lovely one
    showed herself, until the dear image bent   75
    down into the valley, softly, mild as an

angel. And thus he sat there one morning
a corpse and even then the pale face looked
toward the window.   80

THE CRANES OF IBYCUS.

To the contest of chariots and song, which
joyously unite the Grecian tribes upon the
Corinthian isthmus, journeyed Ibycus, the
friend of the gods. To him Apollo gave   5
the gift of singing and the sweet voice of
songs; so with his light rod he journeyed
out from Rhegium trusting in the god.

Already from the high mountain crest did Cor- 10
inth beckon to the eyes of the wanderer,
and with holy fear he steps into Poseidon's
pine grove. Nothing moves about him,
only swarms of cranes accompanying him,
which, in grayish trains, are journeying to   15
the warm south.

" Be ye greeted, ye friendly swarms ! who were
my companions at sea ; as a good omen I

take you, my lot is like to yours. From 20
afar do we journey here and plead for a
hospitable roof—let the guest be favorable
to us, he who wards off disgrace from the
stranger!"

And with light heart he hurries his steps and 25
finds himself in the midst of the forest; then
suddenly upon the narrow path two mur-
derers blocked the way. He must prepare
himself for the fight, but soon his hand 30
sinks exhausted; it has bent the tender
strings of the lyre, but never the might of
the bow.

He calls to men, to gods, but his pleading reaches
no saviour; as far as he sends his voice 35
nothing living is seen here. "So I must
die here deserted, unwept, upon a strange
land, perish at the hands of wicked fellows,
where not even an avenger appears for me!" 40

And cruelly overpowered he sinks, and then
the wings of the cranes rustle; he hears, for

already he can no longer see, the nearby
voices terribly cawing. "By you, ye cranes   45
up yonder, be the charge of my murder
raised, if no other voice speaks!" He cries
out thus, and dies.

The naked body is found, and soon, although   50
disfigured by wounds, the guest friend in
Corinth recognizes the face that is precious
to him. "And must I find thee thus again,
when I had hoped with the pine-wreath to
crown the temples of the singer, radiant   55
with the glow of his fame!"

And all the guests hear it with grief, as they are
gathered at the festival of Poseidon; grief
seizes all Greece, every heart feels the loss.   60
In a tumult the people press to the judge,
their fury demands vengeance for the manes
of the slain one, to make amends with the
slayers' blood.

But where is the trace which makes known the   65
evil doer out of the passing throng of people,

invited by the splendor of the games? Are
they robbers who cowardly slew him? Did   70
some hidden envious foe commit the deed?
Only Helios is able to tell, he who shines on
every earthly thing.

Perhaps even now with bold step he walks
  through the midst of the Greeks, and while 75
  vengeance seeks him, he partakes of the
  fruit of his crime; at the very thresholds
  of their temples he is perhaps defying the
  gods, he boldly mingles with that wave of
  people which yonder presses to the theatre. 80

For close-pressed, bench to bench, the supports
  of the staging almost breaking, are sitting
  there waiting the Grecian people, those who
  have come in streams from far and near.
  Suddenly roaring, like the waves of the sea, 85
  crowded with men, the edifice grows in ever
  wider-drawn circles up into the blue heavens.

Who can count the people, who can tell the
  names of those who have come together   90

here hospitably! From Theseus' city, from
Aulis' strand, from Phocis, from the Spartan
land, from Asia's far distant coast, from all
the islands, have they come, and listen from   95
the staging to the gruesome melody of the
chorus,

.

Which, severe and earnest, in accordance with
old custom, with slowly measured tread,
steps forth out of the background, travelling 100
about the round of the theatre. No earthly
women stride in such a manner ; these, no
mortal house brought forth ! The giant
form of their bodies towers far over that of
men.

A black mantle touches the calves ; in fleshless 105
hands they swing the dark red glowing
torch, in their cheeks flows no blood, and
where hair charmingly falls and pleasantly
waves about human brows, one sees here 110
snakes, and reptiles, blowing their poison-
swelled bellies.

And horridly, turned in a circle, they begin the
tune of the hymn, which pierces, heart- 115

rending, and throws bands about the sinner.
Conscious-robbing, heart-moving, sounds the
song of the Furies ; it resounds piercing the
marrow of the hearer, and does not permit 120
the sound of the lyre :

"Well to him who free from guilt and error preserves his soul childishly pure ! To him we
may not in vengeance draw nigh ; he jour-
neys freely the road of life. But woe, woe 125
to him who in secret has accomplished the
heavy deed of murder ! We fasten our-
selves to his heels, the terrible race of night.

"And if he thinks to escape by fleeing, on wings 130
we are there, throwing the snares about his
fleeting foot, so that he must fall to the
ground. And thus we chase him without
weariness ; no penitence can reconcile us, we 135
chase him on and on to the shades, and even
there we do not let him free."

Thus they dance, singing meanwhile, and silence,
like the muteness of death, lies heavily over

the whole house, as if the divinity were 140
near. And solemnly, according to old custom, walking about the round of the theatre,
with slowly measured tread they disappear
in the background.

And doubting, every breast is yet uncertain be- 145
tween truth and deception, and trembling
does homage to the terrible power, which
judging wakes in secret; which inscrutably,
unfathomably weaves the dark tangle of 150
fate, revealing itself to the depth of the
heart, but fleeing the light of the sun.

Then of a sudden one hears upon the highest
steps a voice calling: "See there, see 155
there, Timothy, the cranes of Ibycus!"—
and suddenly the heavens grow dark, and
over the theatre in a dark flock one sees an
army of cranes pass by.   160

"Of Ibycus!"—The dear name touches every
heart with new grief, and as in the sea wave

after wave, thus it quickly goes from mouth
to mouth : "Of Ibycus, for whom we are 165
weeping, who was slain by the hand of a
murderer ! What is the matter with him?
What can he mean? What is there about
this flock of cranes?"

And ever louder becomes the question, when of 170
a sudden it flies like a lightning flash through
every heart : "Notice, that is the power of
.the Furies ! The pious poet is avenged, the
murderer offers himself—seize him who 175
spoke the word and him to whom it was ad-
dressed !"

But hardly had the word escaped that one, when
he would gladly have kept it in his bosom ;
in vain ! The mouth pale with terror quickly 180
makes known the one conscious of guilt.
They seize and drag them before the judge,
the scene becomes a tribunal, the wicked
ones confess, conquered by the power of
vengeance.

THE TRIP TO THE IRON FORGE.

Fridolin was a pious servant and devoted, in the
fear of the Lord, to his mistress, the countess
of Savern. She was so mild, she was so good,   5
but even the arrogance of her whims he
would have endeavored to meet with joy,
for God's sake.

Early from the day's first gleam, until late   10
when the vesper bell struck, he lived for her
alone, and never thought himself to do
enough.   And if the lady said : "Take it
easy!" then immediately his eye became
moist, and he thought he was failing in his   15
duty, if he could not torture himself in her
service.

For this reason the countess raised him above
the whole throng of servants ; from her
beautiful lips his praise flowed endlessly.   20
She treated him not as her servant, for his
heart gave him the rights of a child.   Her
beautiful eye hung with pleasure on his well-
formed features.

Because of this there burned in the breast of 25
  Robert, the hunter, whose black soul had
  long been swelled with evil joy, poisonous
  wrath ; he stepped to the count, quick to
  the deed, and open to the seducer's advice ; 30
  when one day they were coming home from
  the chase, he scattered into his heart the
  seeds of suspicion :

.

"How fortunate are you, noble count," he began with cunning, "golden sleep is not taken 35
  from you by the poisonous tooth of doubt,
  for you possess a noble wife ; modesty girds
  her chaste body. The tempter will never
  succeed in moving her pious faithfulness." 40

Then the count rolls his dark brows : "What
  are you saying to me, fellow ? Shall I build
  on woman's virtue, movable as the wave ?
  Readily does the flatterer's mouth move it ; 45
  my faith stands on firmer ground. From
  the wife of the count of Savern, I trust, the
  tempter remains at a distance."

The other speaks : "So you think aright, only   50
    a fool deserves your scorn ; he who, although
    but a boon servant, has become so bold as to
    raise the lustfulness of his wishes to the
    woman who commands him "—" What ? "   55
    the other one interrupts him trembling,
    " speak you of one who lives ? "

" Why certainly, can it be that that which is on
    every lip should escape my master ! But
    then, as you so diligently conceal it, I will   60
    gladly pass it over."—" Your life is at stake,
    fellow, speak ! " cries the other in a severe
    and terrible manner. " Who raises his eyes
    to Cunigunde ? "—" Well, then, I speak of
    the blond one.

"He is not uncomely in form," he continues,   65
    full of cunning, while the count was turning
    hot and cold at his words. " Is it possible,
    sir ? Have you never seen how he has eyes   70
    for her alone ? How at the table he takes
    no notice of you, but languishes, chained to
    her chair ?

" See there the poetry which he wrote and he confesses his passion "—" Confesses ! "—" and 75
   in a bold manner asks her to return his love.
   The good countess, kind and mild, probably
   out of compassion has kept it from you ; I
   am sorry now that it slipped me, for, sir, 80
   what have you to do now ? "

Then, in the fury of his wrath, the count rode
   into the neighboring wood, where in the
   lofty, glowing furnaces his iron ore melted.
   Here early and late the servants with busy 85
   hand feed the fires ; the sparks fly, the
   bellows blow, as though their task were to
   melt the rocks.

Here one sees the power of water and of fire 90
   united ; mill-wheels, driven by power of the
   water, roll over and over ; the machines
   rattle day and night, the beat of the hammer
   is in rhythm, and malleable under the mighty 95
   blows, the iron itself grows soft.

And he beckons to two servants, points them
   out and speaks : " The first one that I send
   hither, who asks you : 'Have you obeyed 100
   the command of the master?' him throw
   into that furnace there for me, so that he
   may be immediately consumed, and my eye
   may see him no more !"

At this the inhuman pair rejoice with fierce long- 105
   ing for the execution, for feelingless, like
   iron, was the heart in their breast. And
   more intensely with the blast of the bellows 110
   do they heat the belly of the furnace, and
   with murderous longing they prepare themselves to receive the sacrifice of death.

Upon this, Robert speaks to the young fellow
   with deceitful words : " Quick, young man, 115
   and do not delay ; the master wishes to see
   you," he says to Fridolin. " You must
   immediately go out to the forge and ask my
   servants there, whether they have done ac- 120
   cording to my words."

And the other speaks : "It shall be done!"
and quickly he prepares himself. But suddenly he remains standing in thought : "I
wonder whether she has anything to ask me
to do?" And he comes before the countess : 125
"They send me out to the forge; say then,
can I do aught for you? for to you belongs
my service."

And to this the lady of Savern replies with 130
gentle voice : "I would be glad to hear the
Holy Mass, but my son lies sick. Go then
my child, and in devotion speak a prayer for
me ; and if you penitently think of your 135
sins, let me too find grace."

And rejoicing in the welcome duty he hastens
away, but has not yet reached the end of the
village in quick step, when, clear sounding, 140
he hears the ringing of the bells from the
bell-rope which festively invites all sinners,
highly blessed, to attend the sacrament.

"Do not evade God, if you find him on the 145
    way!"—He speaks thus, and steps into the
    house of worship; no sound is heard yet,
    for it was at harvest time, and in the fields 150
    glowed the healthy bodies of the reapers;
    no mass-boy well-trained had as yet ap-
    peared to serve at the sacrament.

Soon he is decided, and he takes the place of the
    sacristan. "That," says he, "is no delay 155
    that speeds one heavenward." Serving,
    he hangs the stola and the cingulum about
    the priest, quickly prepares the vessels
    sanctified to the service of the mass.   160

And when he had diligently done this, he stepped
    before the priest to the altar as ministrant,
    mass book in hand, and he kneels right and 165
    left, and waits on every beckon, and when
    the words of the "Sanctus" came, he sang
    thrice at the name.

Then when the priest piously bowed himself and, 170
    turning to the altar showed the ever-present
    God, in high-raised hand, then the sacristan
    announces it, ringing with a clear bell, and
    every one kneels, and strikes his breast, de- 175
    voutly crossing himself before the Christ.

Thus does he punctually do everything that is
    customary in the house of God ; he remem- 180
    bers it all, and he does not tire until the
    end, till the priest at the " Dominus Vo-
    biscum " turns himself to the congregation,
    and with a blessing ends the sacred service.

Then he cleanly sets everything in order again ; 185
    he first purifies the sanctuary and then he
    departs, and hastens, with peaceful con-
    science, on to the neighborhood of the
    forge. While on the way, to complete the 190
    number, he silently repeats the Lord's
    Prayer twelve more times.

And when he sees the chimney smoking, and
the servants standing around he cries out : 195
" Ye servants, have you done as the master
ordered ? "   And leering they grin and point
to the interior of the furnace : " He is taken
care of and preserved, the count will praise 200
his servants."

With hurried steps he brings back this answer
to his master.   When he sees him coming
from afar he hardly trusts his eyes: " Un- 205
lucky one ! whence come you ? "—" From
the forge.",—"Never! then you were be-
lated in your course ? "—" Sir, only long
enough for me to pray.

" For when I went from your presence to-day, 210
pardon me, I presented myself first, in accordance with my duty, before her to whom
my service belongs.   She, sir, ordered me
to hear the mass ; gladly did I obey her,
and I spoke four rosaries for your welfare 215
and for hers."

At this point the count is greatly astonished, he
is awe-stricken : "And what answer did
they give you at the forge? speak !"—"Sir, 220
mysterious was the meaning of their speech ;
they pointed laughing to the furnace : ' He
is taken care of and preserved, the count
will praise his servants.' "

"And Robert," the count interrupts him, shiv- 225
ering with the cold, " did he not meet you ?
I sent him to the forest."—"Sir, neither
in the wood nor in the meadow did I find a 230
trace of Robert."—" Well," cries the count,
and stands bewildered, "God himself in
heaven has judged !"

And kindly, as he had never been accustomed,
he takes the servant's hand, and, deeply 235
moved, he brings him to his wife, who
understood nothing of the matter : "This
child, no angel is so pure, let him be recommended to your kind care ! Wickedly
as I intended, still with him is God and his 240
hosts."

THE CONTEST WITH THE DRAGON.

Why do the people run together, what sort of a
thing is moving along there with a shout
through the long lanes? Is Rhodes falling beneath the fiery flames? They are
running together violently, and I perceive a   5
knight, high on his horse, in the throng of
men ; and behind him, what a creature !
They drag a terrible reptile ; in form it
seems to be a dragon, with its wide croco-   10
dile jaw, and everybody in wonder looks
now at the knight, and then at the dragon.

And a thousand voices are heard : "This is the
dragon, come and see it ! the one that has   15
destroyed our shepherds and flocks ! This
is the hero who conquered it ! Many others
went out before him to try the tremendous
contest, but none of them was seen to return ;
this courageous knight ought to be hon-   20
ored !" And the throng goes to the convent, where the order of St. John the Bap-
tist, the Knights Hospitallers, have already
been quickly assembled for council.

And the youth steps before the noble master   25
    with modest step ; the people crowd after
    after him, with wild cries, thronging the
    steps of the balcony. And the youth begins
    and speaks : ''I have accomplished the duty   30
    of the knighthood. The dragon, that de-
    vasted the land, lies dead, slain by my hand ;
    free is the way for the wanderer ; let the
    shepherd drive his flocks into the meadows,
    let the pilgrim travel joyfully along the   35
    rocky path to the blessed image.''

But the master looks at him severely and speaks :
    ''You have acted like a hero ; courage it is
    that honors the knight, you have proved   40
    your spirit bold. But speak ! What is the
    first duty of the knight who fights for Christ,
    and adorns himself with the symbol ? ''
    And all those round about grow pale. But   45
    he with manly self-possession speaks :
    ''Obedience is the first duty that makes
    him worthy of his adornment.''

''And this duty, my son, you have boldly ig-   50
    nored,'' replied the master. ''The contest

which the law denied you, with sinful courage have you dared to fight !''—'' Sir, judge
when you know all,'' speaks the other with
undaunted spirit, '' for the meaning and   55
wish of the law I intended faithfully to
fulfill.   I did not go there thoughtlessly to
make war on the terrible creature ; with
cunning and with keen wits, I attempted to   60
win in the contest.

'' Five already of our order, the flower of our
religion, had become the sacrifice of bold
courage ; then you forbade the order to
enter the contest.   But at my heart gnawed   65
dissatisfaction and zeal for the battle, yes,
even in the dreams of quiet nights I found
myself panting in the contest ; and when
the morning dawned and came giving news   70
of more havoc, then a maddening grief
seized me, and I boldly determined to try.

'' And then I said to myself : 'What adorns
the youth, and honors the man?   What   75
service did the courageous heroes render,

whom the songs name over to us, and whom
blind paganism raised to the splendor and
fame of the gods? They cleansed the
world in bold adventures from terrible crea-   80
tures, met the lion in battle, and fought with
the minotaur, in order to free the poor vic-
tims ; nor were they sparing of their blood.

" ' Is only the Saracen worthy that the Christian's   85
sword should fight with him? Does the
Christian fight only with false gods? He
is sent to the world as a saviour, and his
strong arm must free it from every need and   90
wrong ; but wisdom must guide his courage,
and cunning must battle with might.' Thus
spake I oft, and went alone to find the track
of the beast of prey ; then the Spirit re-   95
vealed it to me, and in joy I cried out : ' I
have found it ! '

"And I stepped up to you and spoke these
words : ' I feel drawn away to my home.'
And you, sir, granted my request, and 100
successfully did I cross the sea. Barely
had I disembarked on my native strand,

when, by an artisan's hand, faithful to the
well-studied outlines, I had an image of a
dragon made. The weight of the long 105
body rested on short legs ; a scaly coat of
mail surrounded the back and protected it
strongly.

" The neck reached out far forward, and horri- 110
bly, like a gate to the inferno, as though it
were greedily snapping after its prey, the
wide jaw lay open, and out of the black
depth the rows of sharp teeth threaten ; the 115
tongue is like the point of a sword, the
small eyes spit lightning ; the horrible
length of the back ends in a serpent, rolls
itself upon itself terribly, so that it might 120
entwine itself about a man and his horse.

" Thus everything do I fashion exactly, and I
cover it with a loathsome grey ; half worm
did it seem, half cuttle-fish and dragon,
begotten in the terrible deep. When 125
the image was completed, I chose for myself a pair of hounds, powerful, quick, with

fleet foot, accustomed to seize the wild ox.
These I let loose upon the dragon, incite 130
them wild with fury to seize it with their
sharp teeth, and I spur them on with my
voice.

"And there where the soft skin of the belly left
a spot unprotected against the bites, there 135
I urge them to seize the creature and to
drive in their sharp teeth. I myself, armed
with my bow-gun, mount my Arabian horse,
descended from noble breed; and, when I 140
had inflamed its anger, I quickly drove it
at the dragon and goaded it with my spurs,
and after aiming, I shoot my weapon as
though I intended to pierce the figure.

"And although my horse in terror rears, and 145
gnashes and foams at the bridle, and my
dogs whine cowardly, I do not rest until
they become accustomed. Thus do I prac-
tise diligently, until the moon had thrice 150
renewed itself; and when the animals had
understood everything correctly, I brought
them here on quick ships. It is now the
third morning since I succeeded in landing;

barely could I allow my limbs to rest, until 155
I should have undergone the great task.

"For recent havoc in the country stirred my
heart fiercely, for lately some one found the
shepherds, who had lost their way near 160
the swamp, all mangled. I quickly decide
on the deed, taking counsel only from my
heart. Quickly do I instruct my servants,
mount my tried horse, and accompanied by 165
my fearless dogs, I ride against my foe,
courageously, on secret paths, where there
was no witness to my deed.

"You, sir, know the little church which the 170
bold spirit of the master built high on the
crest of a rocky mount. Despicable does it
seem, small and poor, but it encloses a mir-
acle, the mother with the child Jesus, to 175
whom the three kings gave presents. On
thrice thirty steps the pilgrim climbs the
steep height; but, when he has reached it,
though dizzy, yet the nearness of his Sa- 180
viour refreshes him.

"Far into the rock upon which it stands there
　is a blasted grotto, moistened by the dew of
　the neighboring moor, whither the sun does
　not send its light.　Here the dragon dwelt; 185
　and day and night, lay looking for its prey.
　Thus, like the dragon of hell, he kept watch
　at the foot of the house of God ; and if the
　pilgrim came and turned into the lane of 190
　misfortune, the reptile burst forth from his
　lair, and carried him away to be eaten.

"Then I climbed up the rock before beginning
　the difficult contest.　I knelt down before 195
　the child Christ, and cleansed my soul
　from sin.　Finally, in the sanctuary, I
　girded on my polished adorning weapons,
　armed my right hand with the spear, and 200
　climbed down to the battle.　The band of
　servants remains behind ; in parting I give
　orders, and quickly swing myself upon my
　horse, and consign my soul to God.

"Hardly do I find myself on level ground, when 205
　quickly my dogs begin to bark.　My horse

anxiously begins to pant, and rears and will
not move ; for nearby, rolled into a ball, lies 210
the horrible figure of the enemy, sunning
itself on the warm ground. The quick dogs
stir him up, but with the speed of arrows
they turn themselves when it yawns and
parts its jaws, and sends forth its poisonous 215
breath, and howls, whining like a jackal.

"'But quickly do I renew their courage ; with
    fury do they seize the foe, while I hurl from
    my powerful hand the spear at the animal's 220
    loins. But powerless like a thin rod it re-
    bounds from the scaly armor, and before I
    had renewed my thrust, my horse rears, and
    shies at the horrible look, and at the emis- 225
    sion of its poisonous breath, and with terror
    it springs backward, and now my fate was
    sealed—

" Then I quickly swing myself from my horse,
    in haste is the blade of my sword bare ; but 230
    all my blows in vain bore through the rock-

like armor. And raging, it has thrown me
to the ground with the power of its tail ;
already I see its gaping jaws, and it makes 235
for me with grim teeth, when my dogs,
burning with fury, hurl themselves with
furious bites at its belly, so that it stood
still, howling, rent by terrible pain.   240

" And, before it frees itself from their bites, I
quickly raise myself, perceive the exposed
part of my foe, and push the steel deep into
his vitals, sending it in even to the hilt ; 245
black spurts the jet of blood.   It sinks down
and in its fall it buries me beneath the giant
form of its body, so that my consciousness
quickly leaves me. And when I awake, 250
newly strengthened, I see   my servants
standing round about me, and the dragon
lying dead in his blood."

The pent-up storm of applause now frees the
heart of every listener, as soon as the knight 255
has spoken these words ; and ten times
broken on the vault, the sound of the
mingled voices rolls along, roaring in an echo.

Even the sons of the order themselves de-
mand loudly that the hero's brow be crowned, 260
and greatly does the crowd desire to show
him to the people in a blazing triumph.
Then the master knits his brow severely and
orders silence.

And speaks : "The dragon which devasted this 265
land you slew with courageous hand ; a god
have you become to the people, a foe you
have come back to the order, and your heart
gave birth to a worse worm than this dragon 270
was. The serpent which poisons the heart,
which brings forth discord and destruction,
is the disobedient spirit which boldly re-
volts against obedience, and tears the sacred 275
bonds of order ; for it is that which destroys
the world.

"The Mameluke, too, shows courage, but the
Christian's adornment is obedience ; for
there where the Master in His greatness 280
walked in the guise of a servant, there upon
sacred ground the fathers founded this order
to fulfill the most difficult of duties, to con-

quer the will. Empty fame has moved you, 285
therefore depart from my sight! For who-
soever does not carry the Lord's yoke cannot adorn himself with the cross."

The multitude bursts out in a tumult, a tre- 290
mendous storm moves the house, and all
the brothers plead for grace. But the
youth looks down in silence, without a word
he lays off the robe, kisses the master's severe hand, and departs, and he follows him 295
with his gaze; then lovingly he calls him
back, and speaks: "Embrace me, my son!
You succeeded in the more difficult contest.
Take this cross. It is the reward of hu- 300
mility, which has conquered itself."

THE BOND.

To Dionysus, the tyrant, crept Mœros, with a
dagger in his garment. But the officers
put him in bonds. "What were you about
to do with the dagger, speak!" the tyrant 5
addresses him threateningly.—"Free the
city from its tyrant!"—"That shall you
repent upon the cross."

"I am prepared to die," says he, "and ask not
for my life.   But if you are willing to grant   10
me a favor, I ask for three days' time, till I
may see my sister united to her husband ; I
will leave my friend as pledge : him you
may slay, if I escape."

Then the king smiles with deep cunning and   15
speaks after a brief thought : "I will grant
you three days ; but mind you, if the time
be past, before you are again returned to
me, then he must die in your place, but   20
your sentence shall be revoked."

Then he approaches his friend : "For my sinful
attempt, the king commands that I shall
forfeit my life upon the cross ; but he is   25
willing to grant me three days' time, until I
shall have united my sister to her husband ;
so you remain with the king as a pledge,
until I come to relieve your bonds."

And silently the faithful friend embraces him,
then delivers himself to the tyrant ; but the   30
other goes away.   And before the sky grew

red on the third morning, he has speedily
united the sister with her husband, and
hastens home with careworn heart, so as   35
not to miss by a furlong.

Then endless rain pours down, and from the
mountains rush the streams, the brooks and
streams begin to swell ; and he comes with
his wanderer's staff to the shore.   Then the   40
whirlpool tears away the bridge, and with a
roar as of thunder the billows strain the
cracking bows of the arch.

Comfortless, he wanders at the edge of the
shore ; but as far as he can see or look or
send his calling voice, no boat sets out from   45
the safe shore to take him over to the wished-
for land.   No boatman directs the ferry,
and the wild stream becomes a sea.

Then he sinks to his knees on the shore and   50
weeps and pleads, his hands raised up to
Zeus : "O stop the tumult of the storm !
The hours are hastening, the sun stands at
the zenith, and if it goes down and I cannot   55
reach the city, my friend must die for me."

But the increasing fury of the storm renews
   itself, and wave on wave runs by, and hour
   upon hour flies on. Then terror drives him 60
   forward, he takes courage, plunges into the
   roaring flood, and parts with powerful arms
   the water, and a god takes pity.

He makes the shore and hastens away thanking 65
   the protecting divinity ; then a robber band
   breaks forth from the night-like darkness
   of the forest, blocking his path, threatening
   murder, and delaying the wanderer's haste
   with menacing clubs.   70

" What would you do ? " he cries, pale with
   terror. " I have naught but my life, and that
   I must give to the king ! " He tears from
   the nearest his club : " For the sake of my 75
   friend have pity ! " cries he. And three of
   them he lays low, with powerful strokes ; the
   others then give way.

The sun sends forth its glowing heat. Overcome by the endless toil his knees give way. 80

" Oh, hast thou graciously saved me from
the robbers' hand, and from the stream to
the sacred land, only to perish here, parched
with thirst, while my loving friend dies ! ''

But hark ! something near at hand murmurs 85
clear as silver, like rustling zephyrs, and he
lies still to listen ; and see ! from the rock,
babbling, quickly there boils forth a living,
murmuring spring, and gladly he bows him- 90
self down, and refreshes his burning limbs.

And the sun looks through the green foliage of
the boughs and paints upon the gleaming
meadows giant shadows of the trees.   He 95
sees two wanderers passing along the road,
but with quick step he is about to pass
by them, when he hears them speak these
words : ''He is now being nailed to the
cross.''

And terror gives wings to his hastening feet, the 100
tortures of care drive him on.   There in the
beams of the evening sun, from a distance,
gleam the roofs of Syracuse.   Now there
comes toward him Philostratus, the honor-
able keeper of the house, and he in terror 105
recognizes his master :

"Back ! you can save your friend no longer !
So save your own life ! Even now he is
suffering death. From hour to hour he
waited with hopeful heart for your return. 110
From him the scorn of the tyrant could not
take his courageous trust."—

"If it is too late, and I cannot appear to him
as a welcome saviour, let death unite me 115
to him. Let not the tyrant pride himself
in this, that a friend has broken his pledge
to a friend, but let him slaughter two vic-
tims and believe in love and faithfulness !"

And the sun goes down ; now he stands at the 120
gate, and sees the cross already raised, and
the gaping throng around it. Then they
draw the victim up on the rope ; when
powerfully parting the dense throng he
cries : "Slay me, executioners ! Here am I 125
for whom he went bond !"

And astonishment seized the people round about ;
both the friends fall into each other's arms,

and weep for pain and joy. There one 130
sees no tearless eye, and they bring to the
king the wondrous tale. He is touched with
pity and quickly has them led before the
throne.

He looks at them long in astonishment; then 135
he speaks : "You have succeeded, you have
conquered my heart. And faithfulness,
then, is no empty dream. Take me as your
companion ! Grant my plea, let me be the 140
third within your circle."

THE ELEUSINIAN FESTIVAL.

Wind to a wreath the golden ears and weave in
blue cyanea, too ! Joy shall transfigure
every eye, for the queen is passing in ; she,   5
the conqueror of wild costumes, who settled
men with men, and who changed the movable tent into the peaceful fixed abode.

Shyly in the mountain clefts did the cave-dwellers 10
    hide themselves ; the nomad allowed the
    plains, through which he roamed, to lie
    uncultivated. With the spear, and with the
    bow, the hunter strode through the land ;
    woe to the stranger whom the billows threw 15
    upon this unfortunate coast !

And upon her path, seeking the tracks of her
    child, Ceres greeted the abandoned shore.
    Alas ! there no meadow flourished ! No 20
    shelter was granted here, so that she might
    tarry peacefully ; no temple's well-lit pillar
    testified that gods are honored here.

No fruit of sweet ears invites her to the pure 25
    meal. Only, on horrible altars are bleaching
    human bones. Yes, as far as in her wan-
    derings she went, everywhere she found 30
    misfortune and in her great spirit she be-
    moaned the fall of man.

Do I thus find men again, they to whom we
    have lent our form, whose well-formed   35
    limbs bloom up yonder in Olympus? Did
    we not give to him as his possession the
    divine lap of earth, and does he roam upon
    his royal seat, miserable and homeless?   40

Does no god have pity on him? Does no one out
    of the throng of the blessed raise him with
    powerful arms up out of his deep disgrace?
    In the royal height of heaven another's   45
    grief moves them not; but my tortured
    heart feels the fear and woes of men.

So that man may become man, let him found   50
    an eternal compact, in faith with the sacred
    earth, his maternal ground. Let him honor
    the law of the times, and the sacred course
    of the moon, which moves silently measured   55
    in melodious song.

And she softly parts the cloud that conceals her
   from their gaze ; suddenly she stands there
   in the midst of the wild men's circle, the   60
   picture of a god.   She finds the rude throng
   revelling at the meal of victory and they
   bring to her, as a sacrifice, the blood-filled
   shell.

But shuddering and with horror she turns away   65
   and speaks : " Bloody tiger meals do not
   moisten the lips of a god.   He desires pure
   sacrifices, fruits which autumn gives ; with   70
   pure gifts of the field is the holy one
   honored."

And she takes the weighty spear out of the
   rude hand of the hunter ; and with the   75
   shaft of the murderous arm she furrows
   the light sand, takes from the tip of her
   wreath a kernel, filled with power, drops it
   into the little furrow, and the germ of the   80
   seed swells.

And soon the ground adorns itself with green
 stalks, and as far as the eye looks, it waves
 like a golden wood. Smiling, she blesses 85
 the earth, twists the band of the first sheaf,
 chooses the fieldstone as a hearth, and then
 the goddess speaks :

" Father Zeus, thou who dost reign over all the 90
 gods in Olympian heights, let a sign now
 appear to show that this sacrifice is pleasing
 to thee! And take away the cloud from the
 eye of this people, which, O lofty one, 95
 does not yet name thee, so that it may
 know its god ! ''

And Zeus upon his lofty seat hears the pleading
 of his sister ; thundering from the blue
 heights he hurls the jagged lightning. 100
 Crackling, something begins to unfold, raises
 itself whirling from the altar, and above it
 floats in lofty circles his quick eagle.

And deeply moved, the joyous throng of the 105
   multitude falls at the feet of the goddess,
   and the rude souls melt in the first feeling
   of humanity ; they throw from themselves
   the bloody weapon, open their unlearned 110
   minds and receive from the lips of the queen
   the divine teaching.

And down from their thrones descend all the
   heavenly ones. Themis herself heads the 115
   line, measures unto each one his rights,
   plants the boundary stone, and invites as
   witnesses the hidden powers of the Styx.   120

And there comes the god of the forge, the in-
   ventive son of Zeus, the maker of artistic
   vessels, well-versed in metal and clay. He 125
   teaches the art of the tongs, and the blast
   of the forge, and under the beating of his
   hammer is formed the first plough.

And Minerva, towering over all the others with 130
  her weighty spear, lets her mighty voice
  sound forth, and commands the army of the
  gods. Firm walls she wishes to found to
  be a protection for every one, to bind the 135
  scattered world into a peaceful unity.

And she guides her queenly steps through the
  wide expanse of the field, and in her track
  follows the boundary god. Measuring, she 140
  carries the chain about the green base of the
  hill ; and the bed of the wild stream too
  she encloses in the sacred plot.

All the Nymphs and Oreads which follow Arte- 145
  mis upon the mountain paths, when she
  swings her hunting spear, they all come, all
  take a hand, cries of joy resound, and at the 150
  blows of their axes the pinewood crouches
  to the ground.

The rush-crowned god also rises from his green
    wave, rolls the heavy raft to its place, at the 155
    command of the goddess ; and the light-clad
    Hours eagerly fly about to their business and
    neatly do the rude trunks become round 160
    under their hands.

And one can see the sea god hastening also ;
    quick, with a thrust of his trident he breaks
    out the granite pillars from the skeleton of
    the earth, swings them with powerful hands 165
    on high, like a light ball, and with Hermes,
    the quick one, he builds up the protecting
    wall.

But from the golden strings the harmony of 170
    Apollo entrances, and the pleasant measure
    of time and the power of melody (fascinate).
    With nine-voiced song the Muses join in ;
    softly, according to the sound of music, stone 175
    fits itself to stone.

On the wide wings of the gates Cybele sits with
    experienced hand, and she fits the restrain- 180
    ing bolts and the firm locks. Soon by the
    quick hands of gods is the wondrous struc-
    ture completed, and already the light walls
    of the temples gleam in festive splendor.

And with a wreath of myrtle the queen of the 185
    gods draws near. She leads the handsome
    shepherd up to the most beautiful shep-
    herdess. Venus herself, with her charm- 190
    ing boy, adorns the first pair ; all the gods
    bring gifts, and bless the married couple.

And the new citizens, led in by the happy throng
    of the gods, pass with music through the 195
    peaceful open door ; and Ceres at the altar
    of Zeus attends to the duties of priest, her
    hands folded in blessing ; she speaks to the 200
    surrounding people :

Liberty does the animal of the desert love, free
    in the ether rules the god ; nature's law
    controls the powerful desires of their breasts.
    But man in their midst must rank himself 205
    to men and by his costume alone can he be
    free and powerful.

Wind to a wreath the golden ears, and weave in 210
    cyanea, too ! Let joy transfigure every eye,
    for the queen is passing in ; she who has
    given us our sweet home, and who settles
    man with man. Let our song be festively 215
    raised for the happiness-bestowing mother
    of the world.

HERO AND LEANDER.

See you yonder the castles gray with age, over
    against each other, gleaming in the golden
    sun, there where the Hellespont rolls its
    roaring waves through the high rocky gate- 5
    way of the Dardanelles ? Do you hear that

surf roaring as it breaks itself on the rocks ?
It tore Asia from Europe, but love it does 10
not terrify.

The hearts of Hero and Leander did the holy
    godlike power of Cupid touch with the
    arrow of woes. Hero, blooming like Hebe,
    ever roaming through the mountains in the 15
    noisy chase. But the hostile anger of
    the fathers parted the united pair, and the
    sweet fruit of love hung on the precipice of 20
    danger.

There, in the rock-bound tower of Sestos, which
    the Hellespont, unceasingly foaming, beats
    with its stormy waves, sat the maiden,
    grieving alone, looking over to the coast of 25
    Abydos, where the passionately loved one
    dwells.   Alas ! to the distant strand there
    is no bridge, and no vessel pushes from the
    shore ; but love found the way.   30

On the small earth's path it guides with secure
thread ; even the foolish one it makes clever ;
it bends the wild animals to the yoke, it spans   35
the fire-breathing oxen to the diamond plow.
even the Styx, which flows with many waters,
does not shut out the daring one ; with
power it tears away the loved one from   40
Pluto's dark abode.

And through the watery floods, too, it urges on
the courage of Leander, with the fiery glow
of longing.   When the bright gleam of the
day fades, the bold swimmer plunges into   45
the dark flood of the Pontus, parts with
powerful arm the waters, as he makes for
the dear shore, where, gleaming on the high
balcony, the torch's bright flame beckons   50
him.

And in the tender arms of love he may grow
warm again after the difficult passage, and

may receive the reward of the gods, which, 55
in blessed embrace, love has saved for him,
until tarrying, Aurora wakes him out of his
dreams of bliss and startles him into the cold
bed of the sea, out of the lap of love. 60

And thus quickly did thirty suns flit by for the
happy pair in the stealing of hidden pleas-
ures, like the sweet enjoyment of the bridal
night which the gods themselves envy, ever 65
new and ever verdant. He has never tasted
of happiness, who does not steal and break
off the fruit of heaven at the gloomy edge
of the river of destruction. 70

Hesper and Aurora, changing places, went up
and down on the heaven's bow. But the
happy ones saw not the adorning leaves
falling and the grim winter drawing nigh, 75
from the icy halls of the north. Joyfully
did they see the ever shorter course of the

day, and foolishly they offered thanks to
Zeus for the longer bliss of the nights.   80

And already did the length of night and day
    equal each other in the heavens, and the
    fair maiden stood waiting on the stony
    ground and saw the horses of the sun racing   85
    down to the edge of the sky. The sea lay
    calm and smooth, like a clear mirror ; no
    wind's soft breathing stirred the crystal   90
    realm.

Joyfully schools of dolphins frolicked in the
    clear silvery element, and in dark grey
    trains, arising from the sea bottom, came   95
    the many-colored throng of Thetis. They
    alone were witnesses of the hidden love
    alliance ; but Hecate forever closed their 100
    mute mouths.

And she rejoiced at the beautiful sea, and with
    flattering words she spoke to the element:

"Beautiful god, would you deceive! Never : 105
I accuse of lying the trespasser who calls
you false and untrue. Deceitfulness is the
generation of men, cruel is the father's
heart ; but thou art mild and kind, and thee 110
the pain of love doth move.

"In the barren rocky walls my lot would be to
mourn alone deprived of pleasure, and in
endless grief would have to pass my youth ;
but you bear upon your back, without boat 115
or bridge, my friend into my arms. Gruesome is thy depth, terrible is the flood of
thy waves, but love prevails upon thee, and 120
heroic courage conquers thee.

"For thee, too, the god of the billows moved
the mighty bow of Eros, when the flying
golden ram carried Helle o'er thy depth,
fleeing with her brother, and blooming 125
beautifully in the fulness of youth. Quickly,

conquered by her charms, didst thou reach
forth out of the black abyss, didst draw her
from the ram's back down to the sea bottom. 130

"Now she lives on forever, a goddess with the
god, in the deep water-grotto ; helpful to
persecuted love, she tames thy wild pas- 135
sions, and guides the sailor to his port.
Beautiful Helle, lovely goddess, blessed one,
to thee I plead : bring to-day also my loved
upon the accustomed track !"   140

And already the floods were growing dark, and
she allowed the glowing torch to wave from
the high balcony. A guide in the empty
realm, the beloved wanderer was to see the 145
appointed signal. And it moans and whistles from afar, and darkly does the sea roll
itself ; the light of the stars goes out, and a 150
storm draws near.

Upon the broad expanse of the Pontus night lays
itself, and torrents rush forth out of the
bosom of the clouds ; lightning flashes in
the air, and out of their rocky caverns all 155,
the storms are turned loose, they burrow
horrible chasms in the broad water's abyss ;
yawning like a jaw of hell, the bottom of the 160
sea opens forth.

"Woe, woe to me !" cries the wretched one,
moaning. "Great Zeus, have pity ! Ah,
what did I dare to ask ! What if the gods
granted my prayer and he has given himself 165
a prey to the false seas and to the fury of
the storm ! All the birds accustomed to the
sea are going home in speedy flight ; all the
storm-tested ships conceal themselves in the 170
safe bay.

"Ah, truly the undaunted one undertook that
which he had so oftened ventured, for him
a mighty god impelled. He promised it to

me in parting, by the sacred oaths of love. 175
Him only death sets free.   Alas! at this
moment he is battling with the fury of the
storm, and down into its chasms the angry 180
flood is dragging him !

"False Pontus, thy calm was only the veil of the
   traitor, even as a mirror wast thou ; ma-
   liciously rested thy waves until thou hadst 185
   lured him out into thy false realm of deceit.
   Now in the midst of thy waters, when the
   return is closed, you let loose upon the be-
   trayed one all thy terrors ! "   190

And the tumult of the storm increases, raised on
   high to mountains swells the sea, the billows
   foam and break at the foot of the cliffs ; even
   the ship with ribs of oak did not draw nigh 195
   unshattered.   In the wind the torch, which
   was the guide of the path, goes out ; terrible

things the water presents, frightful things 200
the landing, too.

And she pleads to Aphrodite to command the
    storm, to soften the wrath of the waves, and
    she vows to offer up rich gifts to the seven 205
    winds, a steer with golden horns. All the
    goddesses of the depth, all the gods above
    does she implore to pour soothing oil upon 210
    the storm-tossed sea.

" Hear my cry resounding ; arise from thy green
    halls, O blessed Lenkothea ! Thou whom
    the sailor in the dreary waters so oft has 215
    seen appearing as his saviour.   Give to him
    thy sacred veil, which, mysteriously woven,
    inevitably brings forth out of the grave of
    the floods those that carry it ! "   220

And the wild winds grow silent.   Brightly at the

edge of heaven Eos' horses mount on high.
Peacefully in the old bed flows the sea,
smooth as a mirror, both air and sea smile 225
pleasantly.   More softly break the waves on
the rock-bound shore ; and gently playing,
they wash up a corpse upon the strand.   230

Yes, it is he, who, though dead, does not fail
his sacred oath !   With a quick glance she
recognizes him.   No cry does she give forth,
no tear is seen to fall ; cold, in despair, she 235
stares into the depth.   Comfortless, she looks
into the dreary deep, into the ether's light,
and a noble fire reddens the pale face.   240

" I recognize you, cruel powers ! Severely do
you exercise your rights, terribly, unrelent-
ingly. Early is my course decided : but I 245
have tasted happiness, and the most beautiful lot was mine. In life I consecrated my-

self a priestess to thy temple ; I die a willing sacrifice to thee, O Venus, thou great 250
queen ! ' '

And with fluttering garment she swings herself
from the tower's edge down into the sea.
High upon his billows the god rolls the 255
sacred bodies, he himself their grave. And
satisfied with his plunder, he joyfully passes
on, and pours forth from the inexhausti- 260
ble urn his ever-flowing flood.

CASSANDRA.

Joy was there in Trojan halls before the lofty
fortress fell ; hymns of joy might be heard
resounding together with the golden harp-
strings ; every hand is resting now, tired of   5
the distressful contest, because the noble
Peleus is wooing the beautiful daughter of
Priam.

Festively adorned with laurel branches, throng   10
    upon throng is going to the houses of the
    gods, to the Thymbrian's altar. Gloomily
    roaming through the streets the revelling
    joy rolls onward, and left to her woe there   15
    was but one sad heart.

Unhappy in the fulness of joy, without a com-
    panion, and   alone,   Cassandra   walked
    silently in Apollo's laurel grove. To the   20
    deepest depths of the wood fled the proph-
    etess and in wrath she threw the fillets of
    priesthood to the ground:

"Everybody is joyful, all hearts are happy, the   25
    old parents are hopeful, and my sister stands
    adorned.   I alone must grieve in solitude,
    pleasant conceit flees far from me and on   30
    wings I see destruction approaching these
    walls.

"I see a torch glowing, but not in Hymen's
hand ; I see it rising to the clouds, but not   35
like a sacrificial fire. Festivals I see prepared with joy, but with my spirit of fore-
boding I already hear the striding of the   40
god who shatters them destructively.

"And they reprove my lamentation, scorn my
grief. Alone must I carry my tortured
heart into the wilderness, shunned by the   45
happy, to festive ones a scorn ! Grievous
things hast thou allotted me, O Pythian,
thou terrible god !

"Why didst thou throw me here into the city   50
of the everlasting blind, to announce thy
oracles ; me, with my opened senses ? Why
didst thou give me to see that which I still
cannot avoid ? That which is fated must   55
happen, that which I feared must draw nigh.

"Is it proper to raise the veil when the coming
     terror threatens? Only error is life, knowl-   60
     edge is death.   Take, O take this unfortu-
     nate sight, this bloody glimmer from my
     eyes! It is a terrible thing to be the
     mortal vessel of thy truth.

"Give me again my blindness, my dark, yet   65
     happy mind! Never have I sung joyful
     songs since I became thy voice. Futurity
     hast thou given me, but at the same moment   70
     thou didst take away the happy life I then
     possessed—take back thy false gift!

"Never with the bridal adornments will I crown
     my fragrant hair, since I consecrated myself   75
     to thy service at the dismal altar. My youth
     was only tears, and grief alone I knew, every
     harsh action of my friends wounded my   80
     tender heart.

"I see my joyful companions, every one about
    me lives and moves in the joyous feelings of
    youth ; my heart alone is sad. Spring comes 85
    and festively adorns the earth in vain for
    me ; who could rejoice in life that looks
    down into those depths !

"Happy do I prize Polyxenus in the intoxicated 90
    madness of her heart, for the best one of
    the Greeks, as bride, she hopes to embrace.
    Proudly is her breast raised, with difficulty
    does she contain her joy ; not even you up 95
    yonder, ye celestials, does she envy in her
    dream.

"I too have seen him whom her heart desires
    and chooses ! His beautiful countenance
    pleads, inspired by the glow of love. 100
    Gladly would I with my husband go into
    the homelike dwelling ; but a Stygian shade
    steps nightly 'twixt him and me.

" All her pale masks doth Proserpina send me ; 105
  wherever I journey, wherever I go, the
  spirits stand before me. In the joyful play
  of youth they present themselves appallingly, 110
  a terrible throng ! Never more can I be
  happy.

" And I see the murderous steel glisten and the
  eye of the murderer gleaming ; neither to 115
  the right, nor to the left, can I escape the
  terror ; I dare not turn my eyes, knowing,
  looking, unmoved must I accomplish my
  fate, falling in a foreign land." 120

And yet her words are sounding—Hark ! there
  comes a confused sound from the gates of
  the temple far away : dead lay the great son
  of Thetis ! Eris shakes her serpents, all the 125
  gods flee away, and the clouds of thunder
  hang heavy over Ilium.

THE COUNT OF HAPSBURG.

At Aachen, in his imperial glory, sat the holy
  power of king Rudolf in the ancient hall at
  the festive coronation banquet. The execu-   5
  tive count of the Rhine carried the viands ;
  the Bohemian poured the sparkling wine,
  and all the seven electors, just as the multitude of stars places itself about the sun,
  busily stood about the ruler of the world, to   10
  execute the duties of their position.

And all around, the people in joyous throng filled
  the lofty balcony; loudly mingled with the
  trumpets, sound the rejoicing cries of the
  multitude ; for the terrible time, without an   15
  emperor, after a long and destructive contest
  had ended, and again there was a judge upon
  earth. No longer did the iron spear rule
  blindly, no longer did the weak and peaceful one fear to become the prey of the   20
  mighty.

And the emperor seized the golden cup and
  speaks with peaceful countenance : "Truly
  the feast glitters, and the banquet is great,

all to thrill my royal heart; but I miss the   25
singer, the messenger of joy, who may,
with his sweet sound, move my breast, and
also with divinely noble teaching. Thus
what I have done from youth on, and what
as knight I used to do, I shall not deprive   30
myself of, as king."

And see! into the surrounding circle of the
princes steps the singer in his long mantle ;
his locks shone white as silver, bleached by
fulness of years.   "Sweet melody sleeps in   35
the golden strings, the minstrel sings of the
rewards of love, he praises the highest and
best, whatever the heart itself wishes for,
or the mind may desire ; but tell me, what
is worthy of the emperor at his most beau-   40
tiful feast ?"

"I shall not command the minstrel," replies
the ruler with smiling lip; "he stands in
the service of a greater master, he obeys
the commanding hour. Just as in the air   45
the storm-wind whistles, one knows not
whence it comes and rushes ; just as the
fountain from hidden depths, thus sounds
the minstrel's song, forth from his inmost
self, and awakens the power of hidden feel-
ings, which mysteriously slept in the   50
bosom."

And the bard quickly begins to play and touches
　　his chords with might : " To the hunt rode
　　a noble hero, in search of the fleeting
　　chamois.　A servant followed him with the　55
　　hunter's bow, and when upon his stately
　　horse he comes to a glen, he hears a bell
　　sounding in the distance ; a priest it was
　　with an image of the Master ; in advance　60
　　steps the mass-boy.

"And the count bows himself to the ground, his
　　head bared in humility, to adore with a
　　believing, Christian mind, what redeems all
　　men.　But a little brook rustled through　65
　　the field, swelled by the rushing torrents of
　　the Giesbach, and this delayed the wan-
　　derer's steps ; he lays aside the sacrament,
　　quickly from his feet does he draw his
　　shoes, so as to wade through the creek.　70

" ' O what are you doing ? ' the count addresses
　　him, looking at him in astonishment.　' Sir,
　　I am going to a dying man, who is longing
　　for heaven's food ; and as I was nearing the　75

bridge across the brook, the roaring Giesbach tore it away in its whirling waves.
And so, in order that the fainting one may
be saved, I am now about to wade through   80
the water with naked feet.'

"Then the count places him upon his knightly
steed and passes him the beautiful reins,
so that he might refresh the sick one who
desired him, and might not delay in his
holy duty. And he himself upon the ani-   85
mal of his servant continues the hunt ; the
other one completes his journey, and on
the following morning with grateful look
he brings back the count's horse, meekly   90
leading it by the reins.

"'' God forbid,' cried the count humbly, 'that I
should henceforth bestride, for chase or war,
the horse that has carried my Maker ! If   95
you do not wish it for your own use, let it be
consecrated to the divine service ! For I
have given it to him from whom I carry, as
an earthly honor, temporal goods, life and
blood, and soul and breath and spirit.'   100

" 'Then may God, the almighty protector, he
who listens to the pleading of weak ones,
bring you to honor both now and hereafter,
even as you just now honored him.　You 105
are a mighty count, known by your knightly
behavior in Switzerland ; you have six
youthful daughters ; may they,' cried he,
with inspiration, ' bring you six crowns
to your home, and may the latest genera- 110
tions be bright !' "

And the emperor sat there with thoughtful mien,
as though he were thinking of bygone
days ; now that he looks into the minstrel's
eye, the meaning of his words seizes him.
Quickly does he recognize the features of the 115
priest and he conceals the rushing fountain
of tears in the purple folds of his mantle.
Every one looks at the emperor and recognizes the count, who had done it, and ever
after they adored the divine government.　120

THE VICTOR'S FEAST.

Priam's fortress had fallen, Troy lay in ruins,
　　and ashes, and the Greeks, intoxicated with
　　victory, richly laden with booty, sat upon　　5
　　the high ships along the coast of the Hel-
　　lespont, occupied with the joyful journey to
　　beautiful Greece.　Begin the sweet songs!
　　for to the pastoral hearth have the ships　10
　　returned and again are they journeying
　　homeward.

And in long rows, the throng of Trojan women
　　sat wailing, beating their breasts in grief,　15
　　pale, with disheveled hair.　Into the wild
　　feast of joy they mingled the song of woe,
　　weeping for their own sorrows in the de-　20
　　struction of the realm.　Far away, their
　　much loved land!　"Far from our sweet
　　home we follow our foreign masters.　Alas!
　　how fortunate are the dead!"

And now Calchas is lighting the sacrifice to the   25
  high gods ; he calls upon Pallas, who founds
  cities, and again destroys them, and Nep-
  tune, who puts his belt of waves about the   30
  lands, and Zeus, the sender of terror, who
  swings his ægis, inspiring great fear.
  Overcome, completed in the long, severe contest, completed in the circle of time, the great   35
  city is conquered.

The son of Atreus, prince of the throngs, looked
  over the number of the people who had
  come with him into the valley of the   40
  Scamander. And the dark cloud of care
  surrounded the king's countenance ; but few
  of the people whom he brought hither
  did he bring back. Therefore let him raise   45
  the joyful song who sees his home again,
  and in whom life is still blooming freshly
  onward ! for not all return again.

"Not all those who come back again can rejoice   50
  at the return home ; at the altars of one's

dwelling, murder can be planned. Many a
one has fallen through the malice of a friend,
when the bloody battle missed him!'' said   55
Ulysses, with a look of warning, inspired by
the spirit of Athene. Happy he for whom
the faith of his wife preserves the home, pure
and chaste! For woman is of a false breed,
and the cunning one loves the new.   60

And Atrides rejoices in his newly won wife, and
highly elated, he embraces her beautiful,
charming person in his arms. Evil works   65
must perish, revenge follows the deed of
wrong; for with justice does the council of
Kronos' son dwell in the celestial heights.
Evil must end with evil; upon the sinning
race Zeus takes vengeance for the right of   70
hospitality, judging with impartial hand.

"Well may it be proper for the happy one,"
cries the brave son of Oileus, "to praise the   75
ruler on the lofty throne of heaven! Without

choice does he bestow his gifts, without pro-
priety his fortune ; for Patroklus lies buried,
but Thersites comes back ! Because fortune 80
out of its stores blindly scatters fate, let him
be glad and rejoice, who has won the lot
of life ! "

Yes, war destroys the best ! Let there be eternal 85
memory of thee, brother, at the feast of the
Greeks, thou who wast a tower in battle.
When the Grecian ships were burning, thy 90
arm brought rescue ; but the clever, artful
one gained the prize. Peace to thy sacred
rest ! The foe did not snatch thee. Ajax 95
fell by his own might. Alas ! wrath destroys the best ones.

Now Neoptolemus is pouring wine to his great
sire : " Among all earthly lots, high father, 100
I praise thine. Of all the goods of life yet
the best is fame ; when the body has fallen

into the dust, the great name still lives.
Brave one, the gleam of thy fame will be 105
immortal in song ; for mortal life departs,
and the dead last forever.''

" Because the voices of song are silent in regard 110
to the conquered man, I will bear witness
for Hector," began the son of Tydeus ; ''he
who fell fighting, a protector to his family
altars—though greater honor crowns the 115
victor, still a noble purpose honors him!
He who sank fighting for the altars of his
home, a protector, even in the mouth of his
enemy, the fame of his name lives on.''   120

And now Nestor, the old champion who had three
generations, passes the leaf-wreathed cup to
weeping Hecuba : ''Drink it, the draught 125
of comfort, and forget thy great grief!
Wonderful is the gift of Bacchus, balsam

for the wounded heart. Drink the draught
of comfort and forget thy great grief! 130
Balsam for the wounded heart, wonderful is
the gift of Bacchus."

For Niobe, too, a target for the great wrath of
the celestials, tasted the fruit of ears, and 135
conquered her woe. For as long as the
fountain of life foams, at the edge of the
lips, woe is lost in dreams, washed away in 140
Lethe's wave. For as long as the fountain
of life flows at the edge of the lips, misery is
lost, submerged in Lethe's wave.

And seized by her god the seeress now arose, 145
looked from the high ships to the smoke of
her home : all earthly existence is smoke ;
just as the column of steam moves, all the
greatness of earth vanishes, only the gods
remain steadfast. About the horse of the 150

rider, and about ships, cares are floating.
To-morrow we can no longer, therefore let 155
us live to-day !

THE ALPINE HUNTER.

Do you not wish to watch the little lambs ? The
   little lamb so sweet and mild, feeds itself
   from the blossoms of the grass, playing at
   the edge of the brook. " Mother, mother,   5
   let me go, to the chase on the mountain
   heights ! "

Will you not lead on the herd with the joyous
   sound of the horn ? Sweetly sound the
   bells in the joyful song of the wood. 10
   " Mother, mother, let me go, to roam on the
   mountain heights ! "

Will you not tend the flowers which stand so
   peacefully in the bed ? Outside no garden
   invites you ; it is wild out on the deserted 15
   heights ! " Let them, let the flowers
   bloom ! Mother, mother, let me go."

And the boy went to the chase, and was driven 20
    and hurried away, restless with wild daring,
    to the dark place of the mountain, and be-
    fore him with the speed of the wind moves
    the trembling chamois.

Upon the naked peaks of the rocks it climbs 25
    with easy leap. Through the clefts of
    broken rocks, a daring leap carries her ; but
    behind her, he recklessly follows with the 30
    deadly bow.

And now it stands upon the jagged crest on the
    highest peak, where the rocks extend sheer
    downward, and the path has disappeared.
    Beneath is the steep height, behind the 35
    nearness of the foe.

With a mute look of woe it pleads with the cruel
    man, pleads in vain, for already does he
    bend his bow to shoot. Suddenly out of a 40
    rocky cleft steps forth the spirit of the old
    man of the mountain.

And with his divine hands he protects the tortured animal : " Must you send death and   45
woe even up to me ? "   cries he ; " room for
all has the earth ; why do you pursue my
herd ? "

Hossfeld's Methods

For the study of the Modern Languages

German

New Practical Method..... (Key to ditto .35)..... $1.00

German-English Dictionary, 16mo................. .50

English-German   "   "   .... .50
The two in one vol.. 1.00

German-English Commercial Correspondent........ 1.00
For framing letters either in German or English.

French

New Practical Method. .....(Key to ditto .35)..... $1.00

French-English Dictionary, 16mo................. .50

English-French   "   "   .... .50
The two in one vol.. 1.00

English-French Commercial Correspondent........ 1.00
By a new and simple method, an unlimited number of letters may be framed adapted for all the requirements of trade.

Spanish

New Practical Method......(Key to ditto .35....). $1.00

Spanish to learn English....(Key to ditto .35).... 1.00

English-Spanish Commercial Correspondent........ 1.00
How to compose letters either in Spanish or English. Enlarged edition, with a vocab. of technical expressions.

Italian

New Practical Method.. ..(Key to ditto .35) $1.00

Polyglot Correspondent, pocket size.............. $2.00
To enable tourists or business men to compose letters in any of the four languages.

Dictionaries—The Handy Series

Scholarship modern, and really beautiful print.

Spanish-English and English-Spanish, 474 pages... $1.00

Italian-English and English-Italian, 428 pages 1.00

HINDS & NOBLE

4 Cooper Institute   ·   ·   ·   New York City

Hossfeld Methods.—German, French.

A. Mattice, *Seymour Smith Institute, Pine Plains, N. Y.:* Our German teacher likes Hossfeld's book and would like to use it. The obstacle in the way is, the class was organized two weeks ago and have just been provided with new books, ... Method. We do not like to put the pupils to more expense. If you would be willing to exchange even, book for book, we would adopt your book. (*Of course we are prepared to make satisfactory arrangements in such cases. A. H. & Co.*)

Edw. S. Joynes, *Professor of Modern Languages (Author of Joynes-Otto German and French Series), South Carolina College, Columbia, S. C.:* The Hossfeld books I regard as the best of all the new "Methods" I have seen for the study of French and German. They seem to me to be at once reasonable and practical.

D. Murdoch, *Teacher of French, St. Agatha's School, Springfield, Ill.:* Hossfeld's French Method is more practical than any of the other methods. I consider the feature of the translations specially commendable. I shall use it with the next class that begins French with me.

H. P. Davidson, *President, The Northwestern Military Academy (Incorporated), Highland Park, Ill.:* It has many excellent qualities. Its conversations and interlinear reading exercises are excellent features. (Hossfeld's German Method.)

Etta V. Cutter, *Teacher of French, Lee High School, Lee, Mass.:* I am convinced that it (Hossfeld's French Method) is a very desirable method to follow. * * * I have liked .... very much, but believe that I would prefer the Hossfeld to use with my Worman's.

Hossfeld Methods.—German, French.

Prof. H. T. J. Ludwig, *North Carolina College, Mt. Pleasant, N. C.:* Please send——copies Hossfeld's New French Method, at rate for first introduction. I wish also to examine the complete series with a view to introducing the full course here.

A. V. Miller, *A.M., Ph.B., Ohio Normal University, Ada, Ohio:* Hossfeld's French Method shows its author to be an able, practical teacher, who has manifestly made himself thoroughly master of his subject.

Prof. W. H. Rosenstengel, *Madison, Wisconsin. :* I have examined your Hossfeld's Method, and have recommended it to those students that are *going to teach* German next year.

Harriet A. Deering, Ph. B., *German, and Principal of Ladies' Department, Hillsdale College, Hillsdale, Mich. :* I am much pleased with the Hossfeld French Grammar. I consider the method most excellent, and also *admirably adapted to the needs of those studying by themselves.* There is nothing better in its line.

R. S. Wilkinson, *Prof. of Languages, State University, Louisville, Ky.:* I have examined Hossfeld's German Method with very great satisfaction and do not hesitate a moment to recommend it.

Geo. Hindley, *Principal Weeping Water Academy, Weeping Water, Neb.:* I wish to express my satisfaction with "Hossfeld's German Method." I am unable to see how it can be improved upon for bringing the student rapidly and thoroughly along in the study of the language.

The reading and dialogue exercises I admire very much. The work must have a large sale.

Wm. H. Zimmerman, *Professor Physics and German, Maryland Agricultural College, College Park, Md. :* I wish to say that I am well pleased with "Hossfeld's German Grammar." It is progressive and natural in method, and interesting from beginning to end.

It is *modern*, and practically suited to the times. Success awaits it.

M. C. Smart, *Principal Stevens' High School, Claremont,* *N. H.:* I have examined the Greek Dictionary most carefully. I am surprised that a book so complete and so well made can be sold for the price. I shall speak a good word for it to my pupils.

F. W. Hazen, *Principal Craftsbury Academy, North Craftsbury, Vt.:* I am much pleased with your Greek Dictionary, and shall recommend it to my classes. * * * If your French Dictionary is equal to the Greek Dictionary I shall be more than satisfied.

L. M. Dunton, *Pres't Claflin University, Orangeburgh, S. C.:* Please send......copies Greek-Eng.—Eng.-Greek Lexicon ; ......copies German-Eng.—Eng.-German ditto. (Classic series.)

Edw. S. Joynes, *Professor of Modern Languages (Author of Joynes-Otto German and French Series), South Carolina College, Columbia, S. C.:* The volumes are well made and very attractive. I shall call the attention of the students to them and see that our booksellers are provided with them regularly hereafter. (French and German Dictionaries.)

James P. Thoms, Ph. D., *Principal Academic Department, Wayland University, Beaver Dam, Wis.:* Your Greek-English and English-Greek Dictionary fills a want long felt. It is excellent in form, well bound, * * * accurate in scholarship, and is absolutely necessary for complete and thorough work in Greek. Please send me your terms for introduction to my Greek classes.

Our Dictionaries.—Greek, German, Latin.

J. T. X. Tehan, *Treasurer St. Mary's College, St. Mary's, Kansas:* I have had your Greek Dictionary examined by several of our Professors, all of whom speak highly of it. Please forward....dozen copies as an opening for other orders later on. In the future we shall use your dictionary to the exclusion of .... and others. (Latin Dictionary previously adopted.)

D. W. Anderson, *Principal Public Schools, Hughesville, Pa. :* I am very well pleased with your Latin Dictionary. You may send me the other three dictionaries of the Classic Series.

L. M. Dunton, *President Claflin University, Orangeburg, S. C. :* Please forward....copies Greek Lexicon.

C. A. Meyer, *Professor of German, Albany High School and Albany Female Academy, Albany, N. Y. :* Your Classic German-English English-German Dictionary is a gem among the dictionaries. I shall recommend it to every pupil in need of a dictionary.

Henry Julian, *Bookseller to Washington and Lee University, Lexington, Va. :* Send by Adams' Express....copies each of your Latin, Greek, French and German Dictionaries (Classic Series).

Rev. S. Guilband, *Professor of Greek, St. Charles College, Ellicott City, Md.:* Your Greek-English and English-Greek Dictionary has been unanimously adopted by our College board. We will also take a certain number of copies of the English-Greek separate, because many of our students who have the Greek-English are without the English-Greek....About 170 students follow the Greek course ; so we will need a good supply of dictionaries,

Handy Literal Translations. Cloth, *pocket.* 50 cents per vol

Seventy-four volumes, viz.: (*See also* " *Tutorial.*")

Cæsar's Gallic War. *The Seven Books.*
Catullus.
Cicero's Brutus.
Cicero's Defence of Roscius.
Cicero On Old Age and Friendship.
Cicero On Oratory.
Cicero On The Nature of the Gods.
Cicero's Orations. *Four vs. Catiline; and others.* Enlarged edu,
Cicero's Select Letters.
Cornelius Nepos, *complete.*
Eutropius.
Horace, *complete.*
Juvenal's Satires, *complete.*
Livy, Books I and II.
Livy, Books XXI and XXII.
Ovid's Metamorphoses, *complete in 2 volumes.*
Phædrus' Fables.
Plautus' Captivi, and Mostellaria.
Plautus' Pseudolus, and Miles Gloriosus.
Plautus' Trinummus, and Menæchmi.
Pliny's Select Letters, *complete in 2 volumes.*
Quintilian, Books X and XII.
Sallust's Catiline, and The Jugurthine War.
Seneca On Benefits.
Tacitus' Annals. *The 1st Six Books.*
Tacitus' Germany and Agricola.
Terence: Andria, Adelphi, and Phormio.
Terence: Heautontimorumenos.
Virgil's Æneid, *the 1st Six Books.*
Virgil's Eclogues and Georgics.
Viri Romæ.

———

Æschines Against Ctesiphon.
Æschylus' Prometheus Bound ; Seven Against Thebes.
Aristophanes' Clouds.
Aristophanes' Birds, and Frogs.
Demosthenes On the Crown.
Demosthenes' Olynthiacs and Philippics.
Euripides' Alcestis, and Electra.
Euripides' Bacchantes, and Hercules Furens.
Euripides' Hecuba, and Andromache.
Euripides' Iphigenia In Aulis, In Tauris.
Euripides' Medea.
Herodotus, Books VI and VII.
Homer's Iliad, *the 1st Six Books.*
Homer's Odyssey, *the 1st Twelve Books.*
Lucians' Select Dialogues, *2 volumes.*
Lysias' Orations. *The only Translation extant.*
Plato's Apology, Crito and Phædo.
Plato's Gorgias.
Plato's Protagoras, and Euthyphron.
Sophocles' Œdipus Tyrannus, Electra and Antigone.
Thucydides, *complete in 2 volumes.*
Xenophon's Anabasis, *the 1st Four Books.*
Xenophon's Cyropædia, *complete in 2 volumes.*
Xenophon's Hellenica, and Symposium (The Banquet).
Xenophon's Memorabilia, *complete.*

Handy Literal Translations (*Continued.*)

Goethe's Egmont.
Goethe's Faust.
Goethe's Hermann and Dorothea.
Goethe's Iphigenia In Tauris.
Lessing's Minna von Barnhelm.
Lessing's Nathan the Wise.
Schiller's Ballads.
Schiller's Maid of Orleans.
Schiller's Maria Stuart.
Schiller's William Tell.
Corneille's The Cid.
Feuillet's Romance of a Poor Young Man
Racine's Athalie.

Interlinear Translations. Classic Series. Cloth. $1.50 per vol.

Cæsar.
Cicero's Orations, *Revised Edition, 1895.*
Cicero On Old Age and Friendship.
Cornelius Nepos.
Horace, *complete.*
Juvenal, *in preparation.*
Livy. Books XXI and XXII.
Ovid's Metamorphoses, *complete.*
Sallust's Catiline, and Jugurthine War.
Virgil's Æneid, *First Six Books, Revised, 1896.*
Virgil's Æneid, *complete, the Twelve Books.*
Virgil's Eclogues, Georgics, *and Last Six Books Æneid.*
Xenophon's Anabasis.
Xenophon's Memorabilia.
Homer's Iliad, *First Six Books, Revised, 1896.*
Demosthenes On the Crown.
New Testament. *For large edit., with Notes, see special circular.*

Tutorial Literal Translations, 30 vols. (*See Tutorial Texts*).

Cicero Ad Atticum, Book IV., with Test Papers, 50 cents.
Cicero De Finibus, Book I., 50 cents.
Cicero De Finibus, Book II., with Test Papers, 70 cents.
Cicero's Philippic, II., 50 cents.
Cicero Pro Balbo, 50 cents.
Cicero Pro Cluentio, 55 cents.
Cicero Pro Plancio, 50 cents.
Livy, Book III., Book V., *each* 50 cents.
Ovid's Fasti, Books III.-IV., 50 cents.
Ovid's Heroides, 1-2-3-5-7-12, 50 cents.
Ovid's Tristia, Book I., Book III., *each* 50 cents.
Tacitus' History, Book-I., 50 cents.
Vergil's Æneid, Book VII., Book VIII, *each* 50 cents.
Vergil's Æneid, Books VII.-X, 50 cents.
Æschylus' Agamemnon, 50 cents.
Æschylus' Eumenides, with Test Papers, 50 cents.
Andocides De Mysteriis, $1.00.
Aristophanes' Vespae, with Test Papers, 50 cents.
Demosthenes' Adversus Leptinem, with Test Papers, 50 cents.
Demosthenes' Androtion, 50 cents.
Euripides' Heraclidæ, 50 cents.
Herodotus, Book VIII., 50 cents,
Homer's Iliad, Book XXIV, 50 cents.
Homer's Odyssey, Books IX.-XIV, with Test Papers, 60 cents.
Homer's Odyssey, Book XVII. 50 cents.
Sophocles' Ajax, with Test Papers, 70 cents.
Sophocles' Philoctetes, 50 cents.
Xenophon's Oeconomicus, 55 cents.

For other Translations containing Test Papers *see " Tutorial Texts."*

Tutorial Latin and Greek Texts, Teachers' Editions, etc.

See " Tutorial Translations," also " Handy," also " Interlinear."

A most helpful feature of the Teachers' Editions is that, besides the Text, the Notes, and the Translation, they contain also sets of Test Papers facilitating examinations, and Vocabularies with the correct inflections and renderings of all words occurring in the text that because of peculiar significance or difficult construction, suggest special guidance.

Æschylus' Prometheus Vinctus, Text and Notes, Price, 60 cents.
Same, Teachers' Edition, with Translation, Price, $1.00.
Aristophanes' Ranæ, Text and Notes, $1.00.
See " Handy Literal Translation," 50 cents.
Cæsar's Gallic War, Book I., Text and Notes, 40 cents.
Same, Teachers' Edition, with Translation, 70 cents.
Cæsar's Gallic War, Book II., Text and Notes, 40 cents.
Same, Teachers' Edition, with Translation, 70 cents.
Cæsar's Gallic War, Book III., Text and Notes, 40 cents.
Same, Teachers' Edition, with Translation, 70 cents.
Cæsar's Gallic War, Book V., Text and Notes, 40 cents.
Same, Teachers' Edition, with Translation, 70 cents.
Cæsar's Gallic War, Book VI., Text and Notes, 40 cents.
Same, Teachers' Edition, with Translation, 70 cents.
Cæsar's Gallic War, Book VII., Text and Notes, 60 cents.
Same, Teachers' Edition, with Translation, $1.00.
Cicero Ad Atticum, Book IV., Text and Notes, 60 cents.
Literal Translation, with Test Papers, 50 cents.
Cicero de Amicitia, Text and Notes, 40 cents.
Same, Teachers' Edition, with Translation, 70 cents.
Cicero De Finibus, Book I., Text and Notes, 60 cents.
Same, Teachers' Edition, with Translation, 80 cents.
Cicero De Finibus, Book II, Text and Notes, $1.00.
Literal Translation, with Test Papers, 70 cents.
Cicero De Senectute, Text and Notes, 40 cents.
Same, Teachers' Edition, with Translation, 70 cents.
Cicero In Catilinam, Book III., Text and Notes, 40 cents.
Same, Teachers' Edition, with Translation, 70 cents.
Cicero Pro Archia, Text and Notes, 40 cents.
Same, Teachers' Edition with Translation, 70 cents.
Cicero Pro Balbo, Text and Notes, 40 cents
Same, Teachers' Edition, with Translation, 70 cents.
Cicero Pro Cluentio, Text and Notes, $1.00.
Same, Teachers' Edition, with Translation, $1.40.
Cicero Pro Milone, Text and Notes, $1.00.
Same, Teachers' Edition, with Translation, $1.40.
Cicero Pro Plancio, Text and Notes, 60 cents.
Same, Teachers' Edition, with Translation, $1.00.
Cornelius Nepos, Text and Notes, 25 cents.
See Handy Literal Translation, 50 cts.; Interlinear, $1.50.
Euripides' Andromache, Text and Notes, $1.00.
Same, Teachers' Edition, with Translation, $1.20.
Euripides' Bacchæ, Text and Notes, $1.00.
Same, Teachers' Edition, with Translation, $1.40.
Euripides' Alcestis, Text and Notes, $1.00.
Same, Teachers' Edition, with Translation, $1.20.
Herodotus, Book VI., Text and Notes, 60 cents.
Same, Teachers' Edition with Translation, $1.00.

Tutorial Classic Texts and Teachers' Editions—*(continued.)*

A most helpful feature of the Teachers' Editions is that, besides the Text, the Notes, and the Translation, they contain also sets of Test Papers facilitating examinations, and Vocabularies with the correct inflections and renderings of all words occurring in the text that because of peculiar significance or difficult construction, suggest special guidance.

Herodotus, **Book VIII.**, Text and Notes, 60 cents.
  Same, Teachers' Edition, with translation, $1.00.
Homer's Iliad, **Book VI.**, Text and Notes, 40 cents.
  Same, Teachers' Edition, with Translation, 70 cents.
Homer's Odyssey, **Books IX.-X.**, Text and Notes, 60 cents.
Homer's Odyssey, **Books XI.-XII.**, Text and Notes, 60 cents.
Homer's Odyssey, **Books XIII.-XIV.**, Text and Notes, 60 cents.
  Literal Trans., **Books IX.-XIV.**, *with Test Papers*, 60 cents.
Homer's Odyssey, **Book XVII.**, Text and Notes, 40 cents.
  Same, Teachers' Edition, with Translation, 70 cents.
Horace's Epodes, Text and Notes, 40 cents.
  See "Handy Literal Translation," 50 cts.; *"Interlinear,"* $1.50.
Horace's Odes, **Book I.**, Text and Notes, 40 cents.
  Same, Teachers' Edition, with Translation, 70 cents.
Horace's Odes, **Book II.**, Text and Notes, 40 cents.
  Same, Teachers' Edition, with Translation, 70 cents.
Horace's Odes, **Book III.**, Text and Notes, 40 cents.
  Same, Teachers' Edition, with Translation, 70 c nts.
Horace's Odes, **Book IV.**, Text and Notes, 40 cents.
  Same, Teachers' Edition, with Translation, 70 cents.
Horace's Satires, Text and Notes, 80 cents.
  Same, Teachers' Edition, with Translation, $1.20
Horace's Epistles, Text and Notes, 80 cents.
  Same, Teachers' Edition, with Translation, $1.20.
Juvenal's Satires, I., III., IV., Text and Notes, 80 cents.
Juvenal's Satires, VIII., X., XIII., Text and Notes, 60 cents.
  See "Handy Literal Translation," 50 cents.
Livy, **Book I**, Text and Notes, 60 cents.
  Same, Teachers' Edition, with Translation, $1.00.
Livy, **Book III**, Text and Notes, 60 cents.
  Same, Teachers' Edition, with Translation, $1.00.
Livy, **Book V.**, Text and Notes, 60 cents.
  Same, Teachers' Edition, with Translation, $1.00.
Livy, **Book XXI.**, Text and Notes, 60 cents.
  Same, Teachers' Edition, with Translation, $1.00.
Livy, **Book XXII.**, Chapters 1 to 50, Text and Notes, 40 cents.
  See "Handy Literal Translation," 50 cents; *"Interlinear"* $1.50
Ovid's Fasti, **Books III.**, **IV.**, Text and Notes, 60 cents.
  Same, Teachers' Edition, with Translation, $1.00.
Ovid's Heroides, **Books I.**, **V.**, **XII.**, Text and Notes, 40 cents.
  Literal Translation of same, 50 cents.
Ovid's Heroides, 1, 2, 3, 5, 7, 12, Text and Notes, 70 cents.
  Same, Teachers' Edition, with Translation, $1.20.
Ovid's Metamorphoses, **Book XI.**, Text and Notes, 40 cents.
  Same, Teachers' Edition, with Translation, 70 cents.
Ovid's Tristia, **Book I.**, Text and Notes, 40 cents.
  Same, Teachers' Edition, with Translation, 70 cents.
Ovid's Tristia, **Book III.**, Text and Notes 40 cents.
  Same, Teachers' Edition, with Translation, 70 cents.

Tutorial Classic Texts and Teachers' Editions—*(continued.)*

A most helpful feature of the Teachers' Editions is that, besides the Text, the Notes, and the Translation, they contain also sets of Test Papers facilitating examinations, and Vocabularies with the correct inflections and renderings of all words occurring in the text that because of peculiar significance or difficult construction, suggest special guidance.

Plato's Phaedo, Text and Notes, 80 cents.
  See " Handy Literal Translation," 50 cents.
Sallust's Catiline, Text and Notes, 60 cents.
  Same, Teachers' Edition, with Translation, 90 cents.
Sophocles' Ajax, Text and Notes, $1.00.
  Literal Translation, with Test Papers, 70 cents.
Sophocles' Antigone, Text and Notes, 40 cents.
  Same, Teachers' Edition, with Translation, 70 cents.
Sophocles' Electra, Text and Notes, 80 cents.
  Same, Teachers' Edition, with Translation, $1.20.
Tacitus' Annals, **Book I.**, Text and Notes, 60 cents.
  Same, Teachers' Edition, with Translation, $1.00.
Tacitus' Annals, **Book II.**, Text and Notes, 60 cents.
  See " Handy Literal Translation,' 50 cents.
Tacitus' Histories, **Book I.**, Text and Notes, 60 cents.
  Same, Teachers' Edition, with Translation, $1.00.
Terence's Adelphi, Text and Notes, $1.00.
  See "Handy Literal Translation," 50 cents.
Thucydides, **Book I.**, Notes and Test Papers only, 40 cents.
Thucydides, **Book VII.**, Text and Notes, 60 cents.
  See "Handy Literal Translation," 50 cents.
Vergil's Eclogues, Text and Notes, $1.00.
  Same, Teachers' Edition, with Translation, $1.40.
Vergil's Georgics, **Books I., II.**, Text and Notes, $1.00.
  Same, Teachers' Edition, with Translation, $1.40.
Vergil's Aeneid, **Book I.**, Text and Notes, 40 cents.
  Same, Teachers' Edition, with Translation, 70 cents.
  See "Handy" Translation, 50 cents; *"Interlinear,"* $1.50.
Vergil's Aeneid, **Book III.**, Text and Notes, 40 cents.
  Same, Teachers' Edition, with Translation, 70 cents.
Vergil's Aeneid, **Book V.**, Text and Notes, 40 cents.
  Same, Teachers' Edition, with Translation, 70 cents.
Vergil's Aeneid, **Book VI.**, Text and Notes, 40 cents.
  Same, Teachers' Edition, with Translation, 70 cents.
Vergil's Aeneid, **Book VII.**, Text and Notes, 40 cents.
  Same, Teachers' Edition, with Translation, 70 cents.
Vergil's Aeneid, **Book VIII.**, Text and Notes, 40 cents.
  Same, Teachers' Edition, with Translation, 70 cents.
Vergil's Aeneid, **Book IX.**, Text and Notes, 40 cents.
Vergil's Aeneid, **Book X.**, Text and Notes, 40 cents.
  Literal Translation, Books IX-X, 50 cents.
Vergil's Aeneid, **Book XI.**, Text and Notes, 40 cents.
  Same, Teachers' Edition, with Translation, 70 cents.
Xenophon's Anabasis, **Book I.**, Text and Notes, 40 cents.
  Same, Teachers' Edition, with Translation, 70 cents.
Xenophon's Hellenica, **Book III.**, Text and Notes, 80 cents.
  Same, Teachers' Edition, with Translation, $1.00.
Xenophon's Hellenica, **Book IV.**, Text and Notes, 80 cents.
  See "Handy Literal Translation," 50 cents.
Xenophon's Oeconomicus, Text and Notes, $1.20.
  Same, Teachers' Edition, with Translation, $1.60.

UNIVERSITY TUTORIAL SERIES

Latin and Greek Texts.   See above.

Latin and Greek Grammars and Readers.
Latin Grammar, The Tutorial, 80 cents.
Latin Composition and Syntax, *with Vocabularies*, 60 cents.
   Key to same, 60 cents.
Latin Reader, The Tutorial, *with complete Vocabulary*, 60 cents.
   Key to Parts I., II., and V., 60 cents.
Greek Reader, The Tutorial, 60 cents.
Higher Greek Reader, The Tutorial, 60 cents.
   Key to Part II. of same, 60 cents.

History: English, Roman, Grecian.
English History, Intermediate Text Book of: *A Longer History of England.*
   Volume I., to 1485, $1.00.
   Volume II., 1485 to 1603, $1.00.
   Volume III., 1603 to 1714, $1.00.
   Volume IV., 1714 to 1770. $1.00.
   Extra volume, 1685 to 1801, $1.00.
Grecian History, in six Volumes.
   1. Early Grecian History, to 495 B.C., 70 cents.
   2.   (In preparation)
   3. History of Greece, 431 to 404 B.C., 70 cents.
   4.   "   "   404 to 362 B.C., 70 cents.
   5.   "   "   371 to 323 B.C., 70 cents.
   6. History of Sicily 490 to 289 B.C., 70 cents.
Synopsis of Grecian History, Interleaved, *with Test Questions:*
   Part I. to 495 B.C., 25 cents.
   Part II. 495 to 405 B.C., 25 cents.
   Part III. 404 to 323 B.C., 25 cents.
   Also 405 to 358 B.C., 25 cents.
   Also 382 to 338 B.C., 25 cents.
Rome, The Tutorial History of, to A.D. 14, 80 cents.
Roman History, Outlines of, 50 cents.
Rome, A Longer History:
   1. 287 to 202 B.C., 80 cents.
   2. 202 to 133 B.C., 80 cents.
   3. 133 to 78 B.C., 80 cents.
   4. 78 to 31 B.C., 80 cents.
   5. 31 B.C. to 96 A.D , The Early Principate, 60 cents.
Synopsis of Roman History, Interleaved, *with Test Questions:*
   1. 202 to 133 B.C., 25 cents.
   2. 133 to 78 B.C., 25 cents.
   3. 63 B.C. to 14 A.D., 40 cents.
   4. 31 B.C. to 37 A.D., 25 cents.
   Also to 14 A.D., 25 cents.
   Also 14 to 96 A.D., 25 cents.

English Language, Literature, etc.
Low's English Language, 60 cents
Low's Intermediate Text Book of English Literature:
   Volume I., to 1580, 80 cents.
   Volume II., 1558 to 1660, 80 cents.
   Volume III , 1660 to 1798, 80 cents.

English Language, Literature, etc. *(continued.)*

Dryden's Essay on Dramatic Poesy, edited by Low, 80 cents.
Milton's Samson Agonistes, edited by Wyatt, 60 cents.
Milton's Sonnets, *with Test Questions*, edited by Masom, 40 cents.
Saxon Chronicle, 800 to 1001 A.D., *A Translation by Low*, 70 cents
Chaucer's Prologue to Knight's Tale, 70 cents.

French Grammar, Readers, etc.

French Grammar, $1.20.
French Accidence, 80 cents.
French Syntax, 80 cents
  Key to Syntax 70 cents.
French Prose Reader, *with Vocabulary*, 60 cents.
  Key and Notes to same, 80 cents.
Advanced French Reader, 60 cents.
Preceptor's French Reader, 40 cents.
Souvestre's Le Serf, 40 cents.

Mental and Moral Science.

Mackenzie's Manual of Ethics, $1 50.
Welton's Manual of Logic, **Volume I.**, Deductive, $2.00.
Welton's Manual of Logic, **Volume II.**, Inductive, $1.60.

Mathematics and Mechanics.

Algebra, Tutorial Intermediate, $1.00.
Astronomy, Elementary Mathematical $1.50.
Geometry, Elements of Coordinate, 80 cents.
  Key to same, $1.00.
  Worked Examples in Coord. Geom., 60 cents.
Geometry of Similar Figures and The Plane, 70 cents.
Mechanics, Elem'y Text Book of, 80 cents.
  Key to same, $1.00.
Mechanics, The Preceptor's, 70 cents.
Mechanics, First Stage, 55 cents.
Dynamics, Text Book of, 60 cents.
Statics, Text Book of, 60 cents.
Hydrostatics, Elem'y Text Book of, 50 cents.
  Key to same, 55 cents.
  Worked Examples in Hydrostatics and Mechanics, 40 cents.
Trigonometry; Synopsis of, *Interleaved*, 40 cents.
Mensuration of the Simpler Figures, 60 cents.

Sciences.

Biology, Text Book of, **Part I.**, $1.00.
Biology, Text Book of, **Part II.**, $1.00.
Heat and Light, Elem'y Text Book of, $1.00.
Heat and Light Problems, *with Worked Examples*, 40 cents.
Heat, Text Book of, $1.00.
Heat, Elementary, 55 cents.
Light, Text Book of, $1.00.   Elementary Light, 55 cents.
Sound, Text Book of, $1.00.
Magnetism and Electricity, Text Book of, $1.00.
Chemistry, Synopsis of Non-Metallic, *Interleaved*, 40 cents.
Qualitative Analysis, Elementary, 40 cents.

HINDS & NOBLE, Publishers

4 Cooper Institute   New York City

Dictionaries: The Classic Series. Half morocco. **$2.00 each.**
French-English and English-French Dictionary, 1122 pages.
German-English and Eng.-Ger. Dictionary, 1112 pages.
Italian-English and English Italian Dict., 1187 pages.
Latin-English and English-Latin Dictionary, 941 pages.
Greek-English and English-Greek Dict., 1056 pages.
English-Greek Dictionary. Price $1.00.

Dictionaries: The Handy Series. " Scholarship modern and
accurate; and really beautiful print." *Pocket edition.*
Spanish-English and English-Spanish, 474 pages, $1.00.
Italian-English and English-Italian, 78 pages, $1.00.

Dictionaries: Hossfeld Series. Best clear-type *pocket edition.*
French-English and English-French, $1.00.
German-English and English-German, $1.00.

Liddell & Scott's Abridged Greek Lexicon, $1.20.

White's Latin-English Dictionary, $1.20.

White's English-Latin Dictionary, $1.20.

White's Latin-English and Eng.-Lat. Dict., $2.25.

College Men's 3-Minute Declamations. Up-to-date selections
from live men like Chauncey Depew, Hewitt, Gladstone, Cleveland
Pres't Eliot (Harvard) and Carter (Williams) and others. New
material with vitality in it for prize speaking. **$1.00.**

Acme Declamation Book.   Cloth, 50 cts. ; paper, 30 cts.

Handy Pieces to Speak.   50 cts.

Smith's New Class Register.   The Best.   50 cts.

Handy School Record, or Teachers' Class Register.   25 cts.

Craig's Revised Common School Question Book, with An-
swers. Revised to 1896. Published at $2.25. Our Price, $1.50.

How to Become Quick at Figures. $1.00.

How to Prepare for a Civil Service Examination.   Revised
Civil Service Rules.   Full directions for both sexes.   **50 cts.**

Bookkeeping Blanks at 30 cts. per set.   Five Blank Books to
the set. Adapted for use with any text-book—Elementary, Practical or Common School. 30 cts. per set.

Bad English.   Humiliating " Breaks " Corrected.   30 cts.

Composition Writing Made Easy.   Five grades, viz.:
A, B, C, D, E.   20 cts. each.   *All five for 75 cts.*

Oxford Handy Helps, 25 volumes, paper.   **15 cts. each.**

Hossfeld Methods : Spanish, Italian, German, French, **$1.00**
each. Keys for each, 35 cts.   Letter Writer for each, $1.00 each.

Brooks' Historia Sacra, with 1st Latin Lessons. Revised,
with Vocabulary. **Price 50 cents.** This justly popular volume,
besides the Epitome Historiæ Sacræ, the Notes, and the Vocabulary, contains 100 pages of elementary Latin Lessons so arranged
as to form a practical course in Latin for the beginner, making it
practicable for the teacher, without recourse to any other book,
to carry the pupil quickly and in easy steps over the ground pre-
paratory to a profitable reading of the Epitome Historiæ Sacræ.
Price 50 cents.

Brooks' First Lessons in Greek, 50 cts.

Brooks' Virgil's Æneid, 1st Six Books, with Vocab., $1.50.

Brooks' Ovid's Metamorphoses, with Vocabulary, $1.50.

WE ARE ACTING

www.ingramcontent.com/pod-product-compliance
Lightning Source LLC
Chambersburg PA
CBHW030541270326
41927CB00008B/1472